Facing turbulent times

Facing turbulent times

Dimensions
of a whole person
for these
challenging days

Gordon MacDonald

 Tyndale House
Publishers, Inc.
Wheaton, Illinois

Unless otherwise
indicated, Bible
references are from
the *Revised Standard
Version of the Bible* ©
1952 by Division of
Christian Education
of the National Council of
Churches of Christ in
the United States of
America. Other
quotations are from the
King James Version
(KJV).

Library of Congress
Catalog Card Number
81-50293
ISBN 0-8423-6695-4
paper
First printing
May 1981
Printed in the
United States of
America

To eight special men who, during the turbulent periods of my life, believed in me, sought out the potential in me, and gave me grace and compassion in the midst of my failures and immaturities. As rungs in a ladder, all have been steps of relationships that enabled me to learn of Christ and choose to serve Him.

MARVIN W. GOLDBERG
my first mentor and coach at Stony Brook School who taught me never to quit.

VERNE LUNDSTEDT
my first spiritual discipler when I reached the University of Colorado.

B. FRANK MOSS JR.
a Presbyterian pastor who thought he saw some pastoral gifts in me and told me so.

KEITH FREDERICKSON
who accepted me into his home and at cost to his own privacy impressed upon me the meaning of character and integrity.

VERNON C. GROUNDS
after whose life I have unashamedly modeled my own.

PHILIP M. HALL
layman and physician with whom I have ground out many of the most important concepts of my life and ministry during interminable conversations.

LYLE JACOBSON
whose friendship and association in pastoral ministry has freed me to accomplish many things such as the writing of this book.

and

DONALD MACDONALD
my father, who was the very first to confide in me that the world needed to have some special people for turbulent times.

Contents

Preface

Facing Turbulent Times was first born in my inner spirit
during the summer of 1979 as my family and I secluded
ourselves at Peace Ledge, our retreat in the New Hampshire
woods. In the solitude and the quiet of that beautiful place,
the Word of God came to life for me as I studied the pages of
the book of Isaiah. Once again I was overwhelmed with the
contemporaniety of the Scriptures. The history of the human
race is so repetitive; only the names and places seem to
change. In virtually every chapter I saw the themes and
struggles we face in our Western civilization today.

It wasn't long before I began to brood on the similarities that
Isaiah shared with Joseph who had lived several centuries
before his time. I found myself fantasizing on the content of a
conversation between the two if they were to compare
notes on the turbulent times in which they lived.

Later I "flight-tested" my ideas before the gracious
people of the Grace Chapel family in Lexington,
Massachusetts. Their constant affirmation and intercession

kept me going. Later I tried a rerun of these thoughts before the pastors and Christian leaders who attended the Urbana Student Missionary Convention in 1979-80. In both cases I came away convinced that I should keep pursuing these themes wherever anyone might be willing to listen.

I can hardly conceive of any book being the product simply of the writer. Too much support is necessary for him to do it alone. In my case, I have to recognize the support of my wife, Gail, who has always backed me with her prayers and encouragement, not to speak of her helpful (and sometimes critical) critique.

I'm thankful for a staff of pastoral associates at Grace Chapel who (I might as well admit it) often cover for me so that I can get this sort of writing accomplished. And as usual, I am extremely grateful to Dianne Stephens, my secretary, who tirelessly and unprotestingly types my manuscripts, calling to my attention the new words I manufactured and the sentences I fractured.

And finally, my appreciation to the Grace Chapel family, a remarkable collection of Christian people whose support and affirmation make it as easy as possible to be a pastor in turbulent times.

Introduction

The huge jetliner was soaring westward at an altitude of 39,000 feet and all the passengers, including myself, were quite comfortable having just finished one of the airline's better meals. It was then that the serenity of the moment was interrupted with the voice of the pilot,

Ladies and gentlemen, this is the captain speaking. Some of the planes just ahead of us are reporting a considerable amount of turbulence, and they advise us that the choppy air will be with us for fifteen minutes or so. I'm going to ask you to return to your seats and fasten your seat belts. We'll try to make the flight as comfortable as possible, but so as to avoid any potential danger, please stay in your seats until the seatbelt sign is turned off.

Soon we all felt the turbulence the pilot had warned about. Even the most experienced of us began to feel a bit unsettled. Would the wings snap off? Would the airplane be thrown into some sort of spin? Would a sharp jolt cause us to lose an engine? Probably not, but it was a time to think, to wonder.

It was the sensation of those moments five miles above the earth that I recalled when I picked up a copy of Peter Drucker's new book, *Managing in Turbulent Times*. Turbulent times? That was Drucker's analysis of the years just ahead in our world. A time of historically "choppy air." A period in which things would become increasingly less predictable, where people would need to be prepared for surprises.

In turbulent times, Peter Drucker said that organizations need to think hard about survival, and that demands an ability to know the extent of one's resources and how to point them in the proper direction. It means, to use his words, "sloughing off" parts of an organization's structure that are not productive. And it means making large investments in programs and people that will maximize an organization's strength and productivity. All of that calls for careful and ruthless analysis, perceptive and bold leadership, and strong convictions about the purpose and meaning of what one is pursuing.

When Peter Drucker calls the eighties and nineties turbulent times, he picks an apt term to describe our future. All the evidence undergirds his prediction. As a business consultant, he looks at the times and asks hard questions about the sort of manager and the style of management which will be necessary to keep business strong and healthy.

But when I think of turbulent times, I am pressed to wonder about the sort of man or woman and the style of leadership which will produce strong families, prosperous congregations, and healthy communities. In this generation I see many who are spokesmen for religious empires and organizations. I am listening to effective fund-raisers, program promoters, and media entertainers. I see some who are good at setting up rules and structures. Some are capable of convincing us of easy answers and failsafe solutions. *But I am burdened because I see very few men with a word from God.*

A godly physician in our congregation once told a group of

young seminary students, "When you enter a hospital room to visit a patient, you bring a word of grace; you bring a message from God." His words, marked with frightening responsibility, could be enlarged: "When you enter turbulent times, you must bring a word of grace; you must bring a word from God."

A person for turbulent times must possess a word, a plan, a style of life. He or she must know how to discern the day and give a sense of direction and resolve. Where do these persons come from? From the same place they've always come from: God-fearing homes, vital congregations, the discipleship relationship of spiritual people.

This book describes two such people who also lived in turbulent times: Joseph of Egypt and Isaiah of Jerusalem. Each possessed some outstanding traits that made them people to be reckoned with. At times both were hated and rejected. At other times they were embraced and entrusted with enormous responsibility.

The turbulence of their respective eras threatened to grind them into powder. It stretched their minds and their spirits. At times the turbulence left them stripped of all supportive relationships except that which they had with their God. On occasion, their words made their contemporaries gnash their teeth in anger and frustration. They were accused, slandered, and maligned. They were framed and jailed. But unlike the majority of people and structures of their turbulent eras, they never waivered.

I chose to examine Joseph because his leadership style speaks to those of us who have to grab ahold of organizations and movements, of families and congregations. How did God prepare him for a moment of incredible importance in the history of his generation? And what did he do with his opportunity? And upon what resources did he call when he was in his hour of maximum danger? The answers to these questions are amazingly useful for our own turbulent times.

I chose to analyze Isaiah because his inner capacity to make measurements of the times and speak to core issues is something needed by men and women who must lead people toward spiritual growth and maturity. Where did he gain his sensitivity? How did he take in the whole international scene of his day and keep his sanity? How did he steady himself against the tide of hate and slander that engulfed him?

As the airliner bucked through the turbulent air, I finally sat back and relaxed. The pilot up in front obviously knew what he was doing. And while he could not control the currrents of the air, he seemed firmly in command of the plane. That's the sort of control we need at 39,000 feet. A person who knows how to operate in turbulent air. And that is what we need at every level of leadership in our world where people need a word of grace, a message from God—a person for turbulent times.

PART ONE
THE FUTURIST WE NEED

1/ The track of a tear

A disturbing message about environmental pollution
produced for television features an Indian brave who sits in
his canoe quietly surveying a river bank. The water he
studies is stagnant, littered with beer cans, dead fish, and
the scum of an oil slick. From an ecological point of view
the river is dead.

Having assessed the damage, the Indian looks up to
glare at the silhouette of a modern city on the horizon. As
the camera zooms in on the facial features of the rugged
brave, the track of a large tear can be seen on his cheek. No
words are needed; the silent message of that tear is
thunderous. The viewer knows immediately who the Indian
thinks is responsible for the blight that pollutes his river.

Because of messages like this one, the quality of our
environment has received a lot of attention during the
past fifteen years, something for which many of us are
grateful. The state of the air over our cities, the condition
of our Great Lakes, and the beauty of our countryside

would have been in unthinkable shape today if we had not been made aware of the issue of pollution.

In recent years the word pollution has come to describe a large number of things threatening to the well-being of people and animals. And the word has found use, therefore, among those who have asked questions about the moral and spiritual health of our civilization. Has a pervading pollution of the inner person taken place that may have set in motion a poisoning of the system of living in which we have all grown up?

This sort of question is dusted off every time there is a crisis which reveals a portion of mankind in an unkindly light. An assassination, a cheating scandal, a wartime atrocity, looting during a brownout: these usually cause some people to engage in what is popularly known as *soul-searching*.

The search of the soul. An attempt to find out whether something central to our being has been polluted. And if one could prove that there is, does it mean that the damage is beyond reclamation? The environmentalists have apparently reclaimed Lake Erie. Could the dying soul of our society be revived—assuming of course that it is on a path of terminal illness?

A long list of responsible men and women, over the past fifty years, have pleaded for an all-out search of the soul of our civilization. I am not thinking of the strictly negative doomsayer who carries a chip on the shoulder because his voice is ridiculed or ignored. Like the poor, doomsayers will always be with us.

I am impressed, however, with the discernment of people like Elton Trueblood, a Quaker philosopher and theologian who has spent a lifetime diagnosing the spirit of the age and asking hard soul-searching questions.

In 1944 Trueblood wrote a book, *The Predicament of Modern Man*, which appeared at just about the time General Eisenhower's troops were storming ashore at Normandy. You could call the subject of the book soul-searching. He was alarmed, he said, that so few were willing to do it.

In the introduction to *The Predicament of Modern Man* (New York: Harper and Row, 1944), the author wrote that he was agitated over the possibility that the leaders of the victorious allied nations would look upon the problems of postwar reconstruction as being matters of "treaties, political organizations, and economic arrangements."

But these, he opined, were only "surface phenomena," actually nothing in comparison to the importance of asking what was being said about humanity when nations could unleash a firepower that destroyed great cities and millions of people. Inquiring of the state of that civilization's soul was a far greater priority than a quest for a new balance of power . . . or as it would later be called, the balance of terror.

Trueblood writes from the perspective of a Christian. He is committed to the law that the state of the inner spirit is fundamental in determining the holistic health of a person or a collective of persons—family, nation, civilization. The inner spirit is the *sacred* level of one's life: that place within where we perceive the presence of God, where we formulate our supreme values, where we brood on priorities such as purpose, meaning, and caring.

This inner spirit is the place of paramount action, and it is from here that all subsequent human actions should flow. If this source is polluted, then it follows that all other thoughts and actions which flow from it would be drastically affected.

The state of that inner spirit in 1944? Troubled! Probably polluted dangerously, Trueblood then acknowledged. The greatest calamity of World War II was not its fighting; it was the spiritual problem that was being revealed by the fact of the fighting, and:

unless the spiritual problem is solved, civilization will fail; indeed, we already have a foretaste of that failure in many parts of the world. Man's sinful nature is such that he will use instruments of power for evil ends unless there is something to instruct him in their beneficent uses.

How insightful! The words were written a year before he and the rest of the world found out about the atomic bomb and the ovens of Dachau.

Listen to him again:

It ought to be clear to us that such a task (that of solving the spiritual predicament) is so amazingly difficult that we should employ our greatest single effort in this direction. If we had even the beginning of wisdom, we should encourage our brightest men and women to devote themselves to *the task of spiritual reconstruction.* We should put our best thought into the elaboration and promulgation of an adequate faith rather than into some new machine.

What compounded the tragedy of this matter for Trueblood was that he saw virtually no one interested in the pursuit of "an adequate faith." It was as if people preferred to fiddle while their "Rome burned."

The sober truth is that, as a people, we do not believe we are engaged in a race with catastrophe. We are not aware of the dangers we face, and consequently we are doing relatively little to meet them.

Thirty-five years have passed since *The Predicament of Modern Man* was written, and looking backward, it is fair to say that Trueblood and those who thought like him were largely ignored. "The brightest men and women" to whom he appealed seemed to have thought that the future could be better insured by surrounding us with the legal protection of great treaties, the military protection of great weapon systems, and the intellectual protection of vast educational complexes and systems.[1]

And what of the results? Among the outstanding accomplishments is that we have managed to avert nuclear war. In some places it is almost a statement of pride that we have been able to avoid blowing ourselves up. We enjoy the countless by-products of scientific discovery. Our knowledge about virtually everything is immeasurably expanded. We live a bit longer and are generally healthier.

Among the liabilities: one has to face the growing fractionalism of races, classes, and interest groups; discredited leadership and products; rising costs, lowering energy supplies, a strange economy, and lots of

unsettledness and generalized fear. We have a little of
something called future shock, and we suffer the loss of
disappearing traditions and customs, thanks to things like
company transfers, mass communications, and the
bulldozer.

But at no point could one say with satisfaction Elton
Trueblood's signal that we are facing a spiritual problem has
received a significant response. While we have penetrated
a bit of outer space and tunneled under the North Pole, the
inner spirit has become for most people a dark, uncharted
frontier.

A person's inner spirit has often been likened to the
foundations of a home or the roots of a plant. Homes and
plants need foundations and roots: without them their
future is strictly limited.

Jesus Christ spoke of two men who built houses
apparently identical in size, shape, and usefulness. The two
structures differed only at the foundation level. One
stood on solid rock; the other on sand.

Having recently enjoyed the challenge of constructing a
home at Peace Ledge, our family retreat in New
Hampshire, I think I can attest to why the second house
builder was tempted to ignore a foundation. Foundations are
expensive, time-consuming, and generally unnoticed later
on. Our foundation was poured at the peak of the New
England black fly season. Those flies, the mud, and the
general dirtiness of the job made us brood on how nice it
might be to get on with other aspects of building and
eliminate the foundation. And, as I've already observed,
when a house is complete, no one ever affirms the builder
about his foundation anyway. At least no visitor to Peace
Ledge, that I can recall, has commented on our
foundation, which incidentally is there.

The two householders about whom Jesus spoke
probably enjoyed an equal number of compliments about
their work until the day of the storm. In the midst of
stress, the two houses suddenly showed themselves to be
very different. One stood; the other fell, and "great was
the fall of it." Jesus' point? The spiritual foundations of a
person's or civilization's life are absolutely essential if

there is to be survival and endurance.

Elton Trueblood said it another way. "Ours is a cut flower civilization . . ." Cut flowers are quite attractive when arranged in an appropriate vase. And a house built without a foundation may appear very attractive. Of course the bloom's days are limited, and the beholder of their beauty tries not to think about that. But because the flowers' fading is inevitable the plant people have developed chemicals that we can add to the water in the vase that extends the life of the cut flower. *But the chemicals cannot indefinitely perpetuate it.* Only the rooted flower will endure for the season. Only the building with a foundation will endure the storm.

The two analogies are helpful to make the point. In the thirty-five years since Trueblood wrote of modern man's predicament, there is precious little evidence to suggest that our society has done much to find either its foundations or its roots.

A structure without a foundation can be temporarily jacked up. The bloom of a cut flower may be temporarily extended through the inducement of chemicals in the vase of water. But without stable support and life in the roots, everything is temporary and destined to die.

As our civilization has flourished, its awareness of its own inner spirit has been rhythmic. There have been spiritual ebbs and flows. Spiritual resurgence has often come in a time of desperation where precious things seemed threatened. Conversely, it appears that prosperity, as a rule, has usually prompted a retreat from spiritual priorities.

With each of these swings, however, it would appear that the extremes have been getting wider, and it becomes reasonable to ask if our civilization may indeed be on its final swing, never to return. There is no reason to dismiss that possibility. It has happened to a number of civilizations before us.

The Indian who sits sadly in the canoe studying his river fits the mood of my own spirit. As he loves his river, so I love my world. His tear of despair over the loss of what may have been is *my* tear. In only one way do I differ from the

message he symbolizes. Unlike him, I am also the polluter.
And any attempt to look down the road of tomorrow and
ask how we are going to live with the consequences caused
by today's choices without doing so in a spirit of humility
and repentance is spiritually worthless. In those famous
words of Walt Kelly's *Pogo*, "We have met the enemy and
he is us."

My world is the world of speed, of knowledge
explosions, of communications, of vast opportunities in
the arts, of amazing discoveries in outer space and
surrounding space. But it is a world amazingly ignorant of
inner space, where God speaks and persons listen.

The track of the tear is because of the victims of spiritual
pollution, many of whom at this moment are the weak or
the unfortunately located. They are the first to suffer the
effects of a dying civilization because, unlike the strong
and the prosperous, they lack the resources (to continue
the analogy) to jack up their private structures or
chemically extend the bloom of their flower. But the day will
probably come when the strong and the prosperous will
also face pollution's ultimate effect.

There is a tear for the Kurd in front of a firing squad
who in a news photo is caught falling as a bullet tears
through his heart. There is a tear for the aged person
whose fixed income will not allow enough money for
heating oil this winter. A tear for the deformed child
whose mother flirted with drugs during the prenatal period.
Tears for the over-radiated. Tears for the alcoholic sucked
in by portraits of the beautiful models in magazines who
drink only the best. Tears for the clubbed baby seals, the
whooping cranes caught in an oil slick, and the elephants
shot mercilessly by the African ivory hunter. Tears for the
tortured, tears for the refugee, and tears for the person so
anesthetized by selfishness that these things—mostly
out of sight—don't matter.

There is a track of a tear for my children and, if God
permit, for their children. Like the Indian's children, mine
may miss many things that once were because of choices
being made now.

Could our civilization reclaim its soul? Only through

the transfusion of persons whose spirits are alive, pulsating with the special qualities about which I have chosen to write. With certain qualities released through committed persons, the turbulent times could indeed be reshaped. But that is a choice we have to make. The record seems to indicate that few are willing to do it so far.

[1]It would have been a simple thing to summon comments from more recent sources about the pollution of our age. The words of a Malcolm Muggeridge or an Aleksandyr Solzhenitsyn would have been more contemporary but I deliberately reached back thirty-five years to the earlier works of Elton Trueblood in order to show that the issue of the health of our civilization is by no means a new one. In *The Predicament of Modern Man* the author himself reached back to quote men like Schweitzer, Berdyaev, and Niebuhr to demonstrate the existence of this concern for at least twenty-five years before World War II.

2/ A different kind of futurist

In the television message the Indian surveys his river and weeps. He knows what the water was like once, and he knows that his children will never see it as it should be. Pollution has had its drastic effect.

But speculate a bit on differing perspectives. The captain of a great commercial tugboat, pushing freight barges up and down the Indian's river for profit, would not share the Indian's displeasure. In fact, he is responsible for the oil slick.

Neither would the Sunday afternoon sportsman in a speedboat who zooms the length of the river pitching his empty beer cans at random. And the general manager of a nearby factory that dumps chemical wastes into the river does not weep for the dead fish. It's cheaper, he reasons, to dump his raw sewage into the water than pay for expensive disposal systems.

None of these three would show the track of a tear. They have evaluated the same river with different attitudes, with different objectives, and with different standards of measurement. Consciously or unconsciously they have chosen to accept the pollution as the price of progress or personal enjoyment. They will not spend much time thinking about the future of the river as long as present behavior suffices to bring them what they presently want. It simply comes down to the way one chooses to look at things.

A similar clash of points of view is recorded by Luke when Jesus journeyed to the city of Jerusalem and paused just outside its gates to gaze at the skyline. Those accompanying him were awed by the sight. They saw walls and buildings, the massive temple replete with its traditions, and a commerical center teeming with thousands of religious pilgrims aching to spend their money.

But Jesus saw different things, invisible things. He saw the predicament of an ancient city, and, Luke writes, he had the track of a tear on his cheek.

As Trueblood pleaded with the people of his generation to search their souls during World War II, Jesus searched the soul of Jerusalem. And what did he find? He picked up the signals of spiritual rebellion, the exploitation of the poor, the hypocrisy in worship, the fierce resistance to the quiet voice of God. A spiritual stench from the city seems to have risen up to his nostrils. But the others beside Jesus did not think in terms of spiritual predicaments, and they missed this entirely. All they saw were beautiful structures and admirable busyness.

Luke records Christ's words as he mourned the city:

Would that even today you knew the things that make for peace! But know they are hid from your eyes. For the days shall come upon you, when your enemies will cast up a bank about you and surround you, and hem you in on every side, and dash you to the ground, you and your children within you, and they will not leave one stone upon another in you; because you did not know the time of your visitation. [Luke 19:42]

The Bible student acknowledges that Jesus spoke these words as a prophet. But in the secular world of today we might suggest that he was speaking, in a sense, as a futurist, one whose business it is to take the information of the past and the present and project its possible results to the future.

Jesus Christ didn't evaluate an economy, or a weapons system, or a marketing possibility, but spiritual health. And in Jerusalem he found it wanting. With the foresight of one who is the only begotten Son of God, he knew that this city was planting the seeds of its own self-destruction. His prophecy of coming turbulence came true within forty years.

A person who shapes his turbulent time will have to be this kind of futurist. It will be important to have a *discernment* capability that enables one to see where events and people are headed. And having that knowledge, it will then become important to know what responses need to be made and how to prepare to make them. That is the underlying message of this book: to introduce some men of the past who had extraordinary capabilities to discern their times and the spiritual predicaments of their people. They were, in effect, spiritual futurists.

The futurists of our secular society are not known to make many people happy when they leave their think tanks and share their prognostications about tomorrow's world. Don't confuse the futurists with those who are forever turning out artist's renditions of tomorrow's dazzling homes, airplanes, or mini-computers.

The futurists who have to be listened to are the ones who examine the side effects, the by-products, and the long-term consequences of choices our civilization makes today.

Nuclear energy is one example. More than one futurist has calculated the alarmingly high probability of a catastrophic nuclear "accident" within the coming twelve to fifteen years. Many scenarios have been written describing the enormous damage resulting through the energy burst and release of radioactivity. The belief that something of this sort will happen comes from the futurist's awareness of at least four realities: (1) increasing international nuclear proliferation; (2) the relative ease by which a terrorist group may now obtain a cheap, crudely made bomb to use in "blackmailing" a

major power to achieve its own ends; (3) the possibility of
a crash of a military plane carrying nuclear weapons; (4) the
increasing number of nuclear power plants throughout
the world.

The futurist does not believe in *failsafe-ness*. He knows
enough about human *nature* and human *error* that he feels
compelled to include it as a prime factor in any equations
about the future. He is forced, therefore, to contemplate all
the exigencies if such an "accident" or "incident" should
occur.

One such futurist's scenario posits a nuclear burst of
unknown origin in a major American city. An American
president has literally minutes to decide whether it is an
accident or an incident. If it is an incident, who has caused
it? If it is the prelude in an all-out missile attack upon the
United States, should he not command his own missiles into
the air against all possible enemies in order to ensure that
he has struck the right one?

A fascinating—although thoroughly frightening—
scenario of international war has recently been
written by General Sir John Hackett, and entitled *World
War III: August 1985* (New York: Harper and Row, 1978). In
great detail Hackett writes as a futurist about events in
1985 that lead to conflict between Warsaw Pact nations and
the NATO powers. His vivid description of the
excruciating death of Birmingham, England by nuclear
attack is more than enough to produce the track of a tear.
One closes the book pondering such a war and simply prays,
"This cannot happen!" But there is little in the world today
that could promise that it won't happen . . . by 1984.

Futurism has done a lot to confront us with the
implications of the population explosion. Who has not seen
the mathematical factoring which describes a world
theoretically reaching a standing room only condition?
While it has been comforting during the 70s to see a
measurable decrease in overall population growth, recent
futuristic studies have noted the increasing disproportion
of population growth between the Third World nations of
the southern hemisphere and the Western nations of the
northern hemisphere.

It is only a matter of time before the world will have to deal with the realities of this population imbalance between the "haves" and the "have nots." Third World nations usually possess the raw materials and natural resources that the wealthier producing nations need to maintain their standards of living. Leaders of the poor nations are learning through precedents like that of the OPEC Alliance that they have economic leverage which can force enormous concessions from larger and more powerful states. It creates, the futurists suggest, possibilities for future confrontation not between East and West but between the North and the South; the poor against the rich. Under such conditions, where does the Christian place his allegiance?

The projection of age curves in the United States suggests to futurists that within twenty years there will be a serious imbalance of retired (nonworking) Americans relying upon the productivity of younger Americans (income-producing) at a ratio approaching five to one. Does this presage something of a painful inter-generational strife as the political power of the nonworking overtakes the power of the working? If this occurs, where will our loyalties lie?

The onset of the energy crisis is real to all of us. Nowhere has futurism had a greater role in recent days than in attempting to ask what a population does should the energy supply dwindle to an intolerable level long before we have discovered ways of producing alternative forms of energy. We've already been told that infinite amounts of energy are available through solar, hydrogen, and carbon sources, but that the expense of transforming them into usable forms will alter our economic stituation drastically. Is this tolerable? Do we have any choice? Do we have the resilience to flex with these changes?

Perhaps the most dramatic example of secular futuristic thinking has been the publication of the reports of the Club of Rome, a fraternity of futurists from around the world who have done major impact studies on life in the coming decades.

Among the things which the Club of Rome reports have spotlighted is the complex interlinkage of world systems of commerce and communication. A century ago, the average person traveled hardly a hundred miles from his or her birthplace. Ninety percent of the goods consumed were probably manufactured within a few dozen miles of where they were purchased. Not so any longer.

Today every part of the world is tightly knit together through systems of transportation, food production, manufacturing, currency exchange, energy resources and distribution, and the various multinational corporations whose business objectives are often dissimilar to the interests of any one of the nations in which they are active. The Club of Rome has pointed out with great vigor that should just one of these systems experience a major breakdown, such as climatological disaster for a year or two, loss of confidence in a major currency, or energy problems, the other interlinking systems would soon topple like dominoes, one after the other.

The revolution in Iran in 1979 is a case in point. The ouster of the Shah and the stoppage of oil from Iran caused the world to shudder economically for almost six months. There is hardly a person in the Western countries who did not feel the direct effects of events in a relatively unpopulated nation of the Middle East which has gained prominence and power to the interdependence of the energy-consuming nations upon its oil supply.

It has been said that military experts do not sleep well if they have spent the previous day pondering the implications of the sinking by terrorists of one or two supertankers in key channels of the straits around the Arabian peninsula. Fifty percent or more of the world's oil supply could be choked off for an indefinite period of time. Some sort of power confrontation would be inevitable.

One moves from statistics and geopolitics to "hunch" if, as a futurist, he moves to an assessment of the mood of people within Western civilization. The question becomes one of what we *feel* as we move among people and attempt to sense where people are psychologically, morally, and spiritually.

Most people would agree that we are living in a time

marked by great mistrust of leaders and structures in our society. We know something of impeachment of leaders, recall of previously trusted products, and the disclaimers of once bold advertising slogans. And so the question has risen, who can you trust?

A recent cartoon reflects the public's bewilderment over the failures in technology. It features a DC-10 passenger plane filled with Ford Pintos mounted on Firestone 500 tires being hit by fragments of the reentering Skylab and crashing onto Three Mile Island, the scene of a recent nuclear power plant mishap. The resulting fire would be blown out, the cartoonist wryly suggested, by asbestos-packed hairdryers.

Suspicion is accompanied by an increasing disregard for the principle of fidelity in human relationships and contractual obligations. We are moving toward a point in the mid-90s when more than half the adult men and women will come from single parent homes. Some psychologists, working with this statistic, propose the possibility of many young adults who possess great pockets of inner anger, who seethe over the feelings of rejection that are often experienced in the process of divorce. Anger from such sources is usually later directed at any figure in authority, government, or business. And of course, one wonders about the health of the future family, given this proportion of people from whom past family life had been a disappointment.

Fidelity as a standard of relationship is in serious jeopardy in a civilization which has deprecated the meaning of marriage, which has searched for and found a million loopholes by which treaties and contracts can be circumvented, and which has adopted a mentality best described by the title of Robert Ringer's best selling book *Looking Out for Number One* (New York: Fawcett, 1978).

But the more we speak of mood, the closer we get to futurism as Jesus Christ practiced it. His futurism was built not upon statistical analysis or the mounting of all sorts of options and scenarios. In this case he was a *discerner*, one who looked beneath the surface of things, for the spiritual predicaments of which Elton Trueblood wrote. He looked for roots and foundations. He searched for the pollution of the soul.

And when he saw these matters of the inner spirit wanting, he spoke of them, warning of their implications and calling people to change. He seems to have been most irritated when he spoke with people who missed the signs of a polluted age, which were right in front of them. Angrily he said to one crowd:

When you see a cloud rising in the west, you say at once, "A shower is coming"; and so it happens. And when you see the south wind blowing, you say, "There will be a scorching heat"; and it happens. You hypocrites! You know how to interpret the appearance of earth and sky; *but why do you not know how to interpret the present time* (italics mine)? [Luke 12:54-56]

Why couldn't they? Because their spirits were, for all practical purposes, deadened. The roots and foundations were virtually non-existent. There was inadequate faith. Relationship with the living God had been forfeited. The new gods were false gods. As businessmen, politicians, religious theologians, they were in touch with all sorts of indicators except those which discerned the spiritual consequences of their turbulent age.

So Jesus confronted them, and he held back no punches when he told them their "present time" was polluted. Without a dramatic rediscovery of spiritual priorities through repentence and submission to God's laws, he warned, there would be serious trouble ahead, and it would affect every man, woman, and child. He was right. The end of that age did come sooner than anyone realized.

Assume that Elton Trueblood was right thirty-five years ago when he said that unless we addressed our spiritual predicament, our civilization was on a track of failure. Assume that the present evidences point toward various crises within the next twenty years that will stretch the fabric of our civilization to the breaking point; that only those spiritually resilient enough will be able to live holistically healthy lives to the abuse and pressure of the times. Assume that we are living either at the end of *an* age or the end of *the* age. In the words of the Apostle Peter, many others, and more recently Francis Schaeffer, how should we then live?

When Jesus Christ looked to the future, he proposed a twofold strategy of healthy spiritual living that was balanced, realistic, and took into account the affairs of God in history. This is how he would have answered that question.

His first point was *readiness.* Specifically he was speaking of a spiritual preparedness to meet God: "You know not what hour the Lord will come."

Readiness implied a concern to meet God on *his* conditions. These included, Jesus said, repentence of sin and commitment to his Lordship. Paul would later enlarge on this principle calling to our attention that, in the presence of God, only what a person had become spiritually would endure. Therefore the person whose assets are in material things to the expense of the assets of the spirit has little or nothing to show when his or her life is evaluated.

Jesus' second point of futuristic strategy is reflected in what is called his Great Commission: "Go therefore and make disciples of all nations . . . and lo, I am with you always" (Matt. 28:19, 20). It is a call to enter a turbulent age, not to withdraw from it. Once in that world, the word is *ministry*—to serve—in the hope that in any age the effects of pollution can be restrained.

Both principles—readiness and responsibility—are illustrated in Christ's parable of the nobleman who left home for a trip of indefinite duration. Assigning portions of his money to servants, he said, "Trade with these until I return."

The servants had no idea how long they would be left alone by the nobleman, but they had to live as if each day was the one in which they would see him again. That is readiness.

On the other hand, they had to handle themselves and their resources each day as if things were going to go on and on. And they had to achieve results that would be pleasant to the nobleman when he returned and audited their accounts. That is responsibility.

The person for turbulent times who chooses to be Christian in the final two decades of the twentieth century will have to reexamine both the strategies of readiness and responsibility. Assuming that our age is moving into troubled waters, how shall we live? What shall we say? Where shall we serve? These are questions on the level of the spirit and address themselves to the predicament of modern man.

Evangelical Christians can surely say that they have spoken the word about readiness. That has certainly been a large part of our evangelistic message in past decades to this world. And there have been innumerable attempts to discern the times. Perhaps, however, our attempts to discern the times have not always been with the motive of confronting the effects of spiritual pollution. Could it be that many have been more interested in determining whether or not God was going to bail us out of this mess by ending *the* age?

When Americans survey events in their own world and speak of pressures and stresses, of godless systems and secular mind-sets that must indeed presage the coming of Christ, they often risk the ridicule of Third World Christians who have lived with these realities for decades. What is happening here in North America may certainly herald the demise of our age but of the hour when *the* age shall come, only the Lord knows.

Christians must prepare to live not only with the possibility of the Lord's coming, but also with the probability of his not coming for awhile. And that means that we must call upon a different kind of futurist: the man or woman with a discerning capability who can trailblaze the way—for families, congregations, and even communities—through a period of history that is probably the twilight of an age.

Christians must look to the formulation of a spiritual agenda for the coming decades of the eighties and nineties of the twentieth century. Readiness is not an excuse for indefiniteness. We must put our finest people to work to assist us in discerning the turbulence in which we may live so that we can do it both in a state of readiness and responsibility. Furthermore, our spiritual agenda must not be targeted upon a ghetto mentality in which we withdraw from the world in fear of its pollution. Rather our agenda must make us willing, borrowing from the Indian's experience, to get out of the canoe, wipe the tear from our eyes, and make a valiant effort to clean up the pollution.

The agenda must include a rediscovery of the amazing interior of the spirit, that secret place within us where God seeks to meet and commune with us. From such visits as that, Christians will see new things and understand fresh priorities.

I personally believe that a spiritual agenda for the eighties and nineties will include two essential qualities of personhood, which I have written about in this book. And for each of these qualities, I have reintroduced a biblical character who shaped his times through the exposure of that quality. These two men are not strangers to any reader of Scripture, and the accompanying qualities of spirit will not be surprises either.

I have to confess that these two men—of whom I write in this book—have become my friends. I have come to admire them deeply as I have seen the pressures they faced and the performance they gave. They were indeed men sent from God and they lived *in* readiness *with* responsibility. It is important, however, not to worship them. Doubtless, they had their times of discouragement and failure and we must not fall into the trap of saying that their lessons are only for those who are heads of organizations, governments, or churches. What we can learn from them and their times has to be taken into our families, our friendships, our Christian communion, our communities; on a larger or smaller scale they can be us.

First look at Joseph of Egypt, a man who brought to his times the quality of *authentic charisma* and then meet Isaiah of Jerusalem, a man who faced his times as the *contemplative believer.* They shaped their turbulent times and, like them, we may be able to shape ours.

PART TWO
JOSEPH: AUTHENTIC CHARISMA FOR TURBULENT TIMES

AXIOM ONE
**The person God chooses to face turbulent times can arise from
any source or background. God does not choose his spokesmen
on the basis of nobility or notoriety, beauty or brawn. He looks for
those with sensitive hearts and submissive spirits, for those
who crave for justice and care for human beings.**

3/ Anatomy of a crisis

Everyone was probably walking on tiptoes, frantic to
prevent upsetting the top man any more than he was
already. Those who had seen him that morning had come
away perplexed as to what it was going to take to calm the
man down and reestablish the routine that marked each
day at the palace, the center of the world's most powerful
empire.

We moderns will have some difficulty in imagining
what was so special about a dream. Most of us have long
since passed the day when the significance of dreams is
noteworthy except in psychoanalysis. But in that day of
which I am writing, dreams were paramount above
virtually all other things. They were nocturnal hunches,
and they were the instigators for acts of kindness or
cruelty; they were resources for the ordering of great armies
to march or stand down; they were the triggers for moods
of exhilaration or misery.

And one morning a dream was the issue that

traumatized an entire palace staff and governmental administration. A world ruler had experienced one of those special dramas of the subconscious and his afterthoughts had been disquieting. Nothing was going to continue as planned until that dream was comprehended, explained, and acted upon.

The complication was that no one could satisfy the king with an appropriate interpretation. Simply put, the dream was nowhere near being decoded, and the inner spirit of the man on the throne was in greater turmoil than ever. At such times there is a certain panic that settles in when experts are confounded. Usually one feels comfortable when the people with the experience and the authority say that they know the score and are implementing a plan of action. But there is a contrasting restlessness when it becomes increasingly obvious that the experts are not equal to the task, when they can't perform according to expectation.

The country was Egypt. The king with the dream was one of the great pharaohs of the ancient Egyptian dynasties. And the crisis was an embarrassing one for a lot of people in the habit of looking good under such circumstances.

The old French cavalry was reported to have lived by the motto, "When in doubt, gallop!" And that may describe the prevailing situation that morning in Egypt. One group after another had confidently shuttled (or galloped) into the office of the king (whatever shape it was: oval, square, or round) and emerged with sullen expressions betraying the fact that they had not been able to do the job. The last of them had now come and gone. There were no more experts and the dream remained uninterpreted. This was the peak of the crisis, and no one was perceptive enough to realize that it was only the prelude to an even greater one. The growing turbulence demanded a leader.

Enter Joseph: former nomad and eleventh of twelve sons in a family who wandered the hills to the northeast of Egypt herding sheep. Joseph. former slave and recent prisoner. Joseph: administrator to Potiphar and head trustee under the authority of the captain of the guard.

Joseph: "man on whom the Spirit of God rests."

If the media had been present, they doubtless would have centered their attention on the irony of how Joseph's name came to the attention of the Egyptian court. They would have turned up the chance relationship which had formed between the pharaoh's butler and Joseph when the trusted aide had been temporarily imprisoned on what had apparently been trumped-up charges. The butler had been subsequently pardoned and released, and since Joseph remained in prison, their relationship had been suspended. But when the question of dream interpretation in the palace arose that morning, the butler suddenly remembered Joseph, the prisonmate who had once foreseen his own release through a dream. The media would have exploited the story and filled columns with the tale that would have seemed stranger than fiction. It all would have made, as it is said in the trade, great copy.

So it was that Joseph, age thirty, stood in front of Pharaoh and heard the details of a dream, the interpretation of which had stymied the best. There is no record that Joseph betrayed inner nervousness or uncertainty. Nor is there an indication that he was intimidated by this sudden thrust from a prison world to the presence of the supreme ruler of the land. All the scarce words of the writer say is that he listened and then launched into the interpretation.

Don't fail to be impressed that Joseph was believed. Something about his being and the content of his words had quickly convinced the pharaoh and those about him that Joseph's analysis was credible. He provided the missing pieces of a puzzle that had eluded everyone. He indeed was the man of the hour.

Harvard president, Derek Bok, recently lamented, "There is a very obvious dearth of people who seem to be able to supply convincing answers or even to point the direction towards solutions." Bok's concern over the leadership famine of our day would certainly have fit Joseph's time. And Bok would probably see Joseph as one of those rare and delightful exceptions in an otherwise glum assessment of contemporary leadership, then and now.

The elusive dream had centered on cattle and grain doing strange things with odd implications. Seven head of fattened or finished cattle had come up from the Nile River only to be followed by seven other head of lean, emaciated cattle. What had complicated the situation was that the skinny ones had suddenly turned on the fat ones, devouring them completely. The same pattern had been repeated when seven ears of diseased grain had consumed seven ears which had been healthy and vigorous. The dual acts of strange violence had obviously sent shock waves through the subconscious of the pharaoh. The whole affair had created within him a sense of dread and a strong conviction that the gods were warning of some future crisis that could threaten the security of the Egyptian state and the stability of his own rule. Small wonder the pharaoh had awakened in the morning in a bad mood. And, small wonder he had wanted a frank interpretation. That much was Joseph's job.

Joseph could have begun his interpretation with the familiar phrase, "I have good news and I have bad news." The good news portion would have pointed toward a seven-year time-frame in which the pharaoh could expect a ballooning of the Egyptian economy, an unprecedented period of prosperity. The weather would be such at this time that the farmers of Egypt would enjoy windfall profits. Nothing would go wrong.

But then for the bad news. Severe turbulence! Symbolized by thin cattle and diseased grain, the second seven years would be a different story. Pharaoh's government could expect seven years of famine, Joseph said. No rain, dehydrating winds, and perhaps a host of other negative factors would converge to bring Egypt into a depressing situation of economic disaster. A strange picture of contrast this forecast of Joseph's, but the interpretation is one thing; the implications are another.

Now therefore let Pharaoh select a man discreet and wise, and set him over the land of Egypt. Let Pharaoh proceed to appoint overseers over the land, and take the fifth part of the produce of the land of Egypt during the seven plenteous years. And let them gather all the fruit of these good years that are coming, and lay up grain under the authority of Pharaoh for food in the cities, and let them keep it. That food shall be a reserve for the land against the seven years of famine which are to befall the land of Egypt, so that the land may not perish through the famine. [Gen. 41:33-36]

With these words Joseph gave the pharaoh one thing more than he'd expected. He outlined a package of responses that could maximize the effects of the good news and minimize the effects of the bad. A careful analysis of Joseph's proposal will show that it was both logistical and spiritual in design. It obviously required a person skilled in the art of crisis management who would have but little time to organize one of the greatest national conservation programs on record. The logistics would require excellence in communications, transportation, warehousing, security, and ultimate distribution. That in itself called for some sort of superman, the likes of which comes only once or twice in a century—and sometimes not at all.

It is said that this was the kind of mind that Dwight D. Eisenhower possessed. What had brought him to the attention of General George Marshall was his incredible ability to see the big picture of an enormous army and its objectives. Eisenhower's capacity to play military architect for an invasion force of millions of men and megatons of accompanying material brought World War II to a victorious conclusion for the allies.

But Joseph's description of a special man has far greater implications than the search for a manager or a general. History has given enough insight now to realize that what this person was being asked to do reached down to the spiritual core of the lives of millions of human beings. Joseph was proposing that a nation bind itself to an economic austerity program during a period of unprecedented prosperity—an unheard of thing.

Instead of wild spending, Joseph was proposing heavy saving. Instead of epicurean meals, Joseph was asking for food rationing. Instead of an orgy of profits, Joseph was plotting a tightening of the belt. Only under extreme wartime conditions have nations ever had a record of accepting such stringent demands. But to ask a nation to save for the future when all of the present indicators of the day said spend seemed next to impossible.

And all of this would have to be done only on the evidence of an interpreted dream, a hunch about the future. Apart from that there would be no evidence, no sure thing. The word of Joseph was the only authority. Get people to believe that, give up their right to extra happiness and good times, and you have a condition rarely seen in the chronicles of human history.

But Joseph was believable and the pharaoh was the first to accept the challenge. Scripture says, "This proposal seemed good to Pharaoh and to all of his servants" (v. 37). That meant that the first major question on the problem-solving agenda would be: Where do we find such a man to get preparations under way? The scope of a search for such a man is implied in Pharaoh's question to his associates in government: "Can we find such a man as this in whom is the spirit of God?"

I'm quite sure that the Egyptian pharaoh—hardly more than a pagan by Christian standards—was not referring to what the Christian thinks of as a "Spirit-filled" person. Perhaps the king was so filled with respect for the problem and the kind of person needed to solve it that he could only turn to the sphere of mystery when he asked from whence does such a person come. This kind of human being is not found in great quantities, to say the least. Should he be found, the pharaoh thought, he would have qualities like unto the gods themselves.

One has to assume that serious thought was given to the selection of a person to fill Joseph's proposed job description. Interestingly enough, the search committee ultimately came back to Joseph himself, the implication being that no one in Egypt was as wise and discreet as he had already proved himself to be and that is where the mantle fell. Joseph—aged thirty—was designated the man of the hour. On his shoulders would lay the responsibility for managing the logistics and generating the spirit that would bring Egypt kicking and screaming through an amazing fourteen-year period of time.

Pharaoh's question remains pertinent even to this day: "Can we find such a man in whom is the spirit of God?" A question of equal importance might be: How are such men and women made? What background and experiences produce people who are able to look to the future, decipher the times, recommend action, and then give leadership to it?

As Western culture enters the final two decades of the twentieth century, it is painfully apparent that such people are few and far between. To that point the words of Derek Bok have already spoken. It is not that we lack the tools or even the personnel for bringing to bear the necessary management solutions to the turbulence of our times. We have, as a society, perfected the instruments available for leadership to a level at which a Joseph would never have conceived.

We have instant communications, computers, systems analysis, psychological profiles, capacities for gathering the data of polls, surveys, and other forms of consensus. We seem to lack nothing *but* the kinds of person of whom it can be said—even in the mystical words of Egypt's pharaoh—the spirit of God rests upon him or her.

In general I speak of the person whose spiritual development is dynamic enough to awaken the spirit in others. Specifically I speak of a person anointed by God's Spirit who brings an eternal perspective to history.

Few leaders with spiritual quality have arisen during the corresponding period of history of technological advance. Here and there an exceptional person has spoken, and we have all sensed a different medium of leadership, something out of the ordinary—a Nehru, a Churchill, a Martin Luther King, a Graham, a Stanley Jones. What each of these has accomplished has been in contrast with the normal trends of leadership. They were not those who told people what they desired to hear. They made few promises. They often demanded that people face reality and its alternative choices and consequences. But one sees less and less of these types.

But they did bring people together—often to face great hardship with deep commitment. They spoke to unpopular causes and discouraging situations. They asked little or nothing for what they were doing except that the people they led seek out their own best potential.

And what of their opposites in contemporary leadership? The leaders who depend upon polls to tell them what people most want to hear? Leaders who entertain both in the spiritual and political world? Leaders who make people feel good? Leaders adept in the art of doublespeak? One is reminded of the comment a politician made as he drove away from a county fair, "I had such a good time that I lost track of what I was saying. I hope I didn't speak so plainly that they understood me." What of leaders who are the darlings of interest groups? Leaders who are not servants but "lords"? Leaders who will sag and collapse in turbulence.

Karl Jaspers, the German philosopher, was quoted as saying: "The power of leadership appears to be declining everywhere. More and more of the men we see coming to the top seem to be merely drifting . . . the result is helplessness in a collective leadership that hides from the public."

If we ask what qualities must mark leaders in the eighties and nineties, a good starting place might be back with Joseph. Why can't we draft him again? And if we can't, why not inquire about the experiences and training that made him? Perhaps there would be hope if "Josephs" could arise in government, business, science, and of course, the church.

Where did Joseph come from? Biblical history answers that question in a quick burst of paragraphs that reduce an entire thirty-year period of human maturation to a handful of salient experiences. It is not, of course, that each day in Joseph's life wasn't significant toward the moment in which he would stand before the pharaoh, but the comments of the historian focus on those various few incidents which symbolize the best and worst of all the others. Here are the turning points, the historian is saying, those moments of summation when the character of a man turned on the lathe of God shows that it is closer and closer to the specifications of leadership. They are all we really need to know about the making of an extraordinary person.

The roots of Egypt's new young prime minister are
revealed in a brief study of his childhood and adolescent
years which suggests the first of several important
ingredients that would emerge later. The message is this:
Joseph possessed an overwhelming sense of destiny which
outlasted the attempts of people and the crush of
circumstances to destroy it. This strange drive, almost
mystical in force, cannot be underestimated. We must
accept the notion that it came from God and that it was
there to be fostered and nudged along. We would do well
to study it in all forms of its manifestations in order that
we might see its birth in the spirit of our contemporaries.

Genesis chapter 37 tells the story. Growing up in a large
family, Joseph was quickly established as a favorite among
all the sons of Jacob. While it may have been culturally
permissible for such favoritism to be shown by a father, it
did nothing to engender affection toward Joseph by his older
brothers. This was the first of several reasons why they
grew increasingly irritable every time they saw him. From
this relational seedbed came two themes of encounter
which both set Joseph apart from the rest and made even
plainer the sense of destiny which began to burn
intensely within his life.

There is, first of all, Joseph's commitment to a
standard of rightness in the conduct of work. Having tended
sheep with his brothers, he was well acquainted with
some of the shabby treatment the family business was
getting. Apparently he didn't hesitate to report to his
father about what he considered to be bad commercial
practices. What other brothers were anxious to cover up,
Joseph was not. Thus he wasn't endeared to his brothers
when he countered their false profit and loss statements
with his more accurate ones.

The result? Family hostility. But nevertheless it tells us
something of where Joseph is during his earliest years. He
is incapable of being intimidated by those who are bigger,
older, or more in the majority than he is. A force smolders
within his spirit that indicates that he will stand alone
even if no one else chooses to support him. Today we'd
certainly label him an individualist, the very best of a

kind. This theme of honesty and integrity will appear again. That he was ready to defend the interests of his father shows why he will be ready to defend the interests of both the pharaoh and Egypt later on.

A second evidence that points toward an emerging sense of destiny are those youthful dreams that the Genesis writer mentions. Take, for example, the dream in which he pictured his family as sheaves in the field bowing down to a sheaf that represented himself. When he shared the dream's contents, his brothers were quick to pick up the obvious interpretation for they immediately asked, "Are you indeed to reign over us? Are you to indeed have dominion over us?"

A second dream apparently angered his strongest supporter in the family, his father. When he likened the family to celestial bodies in the sky bowing down to him, his father asked, "Shall I and your mother and your brothers indeed come to bow ourselves to the ground before you?"

If, as some believe, dreams provide insight into the strange workings of the subconscious—where profound thoughts breed before they ever rise to the surface—here is a case worth studying. The themes of authority and leadership are the bottom line of Joseph's dreams. And one could hardly escape the suggestion that a sense of destiny and the mysterious call to leadership is already formulating in the inner life of the young man. While these dreams would never make any sense to Joseph's family for at least twenty-five years, it is easy now to look back and suspect that God was already "programming" Joseph's spirit for the day when he would take charge in Egypt. An analysis of these dreams cannot be avoided in investigating how Joseph is called by God to perform for the Egyptian pharaoh.

The voluntary minority reports Joseph brought to his father about his brothers and the dreams of celestial bodies and sheaves of grain are the extent of our knowledge of his thinking and action during a period of about eighteen years. It is hard not to question the wisdom with which the boy handled himself during these days, and it is not surprising that the response he received from his family was less than enthusiastic. I often wish that Joseph had been a bit more discreet, that he would have matched his high standards of moral rightness with a bit more wisdom. But he didn't, and so we are left to simply smile over the jagged edges of the gifted boy becoming a dynamic man

This sense of destiny toward leadership must have come completely from within Joseph himself. It certainly was not fostered by the circumstances which surrounded him. He was among the youngest of a large family in a culture which tended to acknowledge leadership by seniority. If anyone should have had illusions of grandeur, it would have been the firstborn son, Reuben. But ironically, it was Reuben who would prevent the other brothers from killing Joseph when the arrogant little brother would hint that he had the privileges of the firstborn son coming to him.

A frequently seen biblical theme is reflected here. God often reached beyond the firstborn within families to sovereignly choose men to become his leaders and spokesmen. Joseph's perception of this matter is complemented by the episode in which Samuel, a prophet of Israel, skipped over the first seven sons of Jesse to anoint an eighth, David, as the coming king of Israel. The choice of Jacob over Esau within the patriarchal family is another example.

Perhaps Paul had this theme on his mind when he wrote to the Corinthians, "Not many of you were wise . . . powerful . . . of noble birth; but God chose what is foolish . . . weak . . . low" (1 Cor. 1:26-28). The choices of God make an interesting study, and they are seen at work in the early stages of Joseph's experience.

That Joseph should entertain such a high view of himself is also amazing when one remembers that his family was essentially nomadic, living in a land that did not belong to them, at least at this point in time. Yet from such a rootless background the young boy still had the wherewithal to perceive himself as becoming savior of his family and anyone else who would stand in the way someday.

In the absence of any other data, the assumption has to

be that Joseph's sense of destiny emerges from the implants
upon his soul placed there by God's spirit. Here is the
line of Abraham, traced upon the inner being of a boy who
is rejected by those closest to him.

That Joseph's view of himself endured as a spiritual reality
was all the more remarkable as the family pressure grew
against him. Whoever stepped forward to affirm Joseph?
Whoever had the forethought and perception to see
beyond the indiscretions of a boy's ego not yet controlled,
and see the possibilities for him? Apparently, Joseph bore
his destiny alone. I ask myself if that early loneliness was
not part of God's effort to temper Joseph and to prepare
him for even greater moments of aloneness when he would
be the target of criticism and opposition from the
majority of a population in a nation resenting austerity in a
time of prosperity.

It is worth asking if our present age—within Christianity
and without—breeds people capable of a sense of destiny.
The quality of which I speak should not be confused
with ambition, ego, or the search for control or
prosperity—questionable qualities which we have reaped in
abundance. Rather, destiny is a quality born within the
human spirit, conceived there by the Holy Spirit of God. It
is a quality which instinctively discerns conditions and
circumstances, determines appropriate responses, and
directs through word and deed the efforts of people toward
the superior alternative.

Destiny—an awareness of one's place and responsibility—
is not an instantly created matter. It seems almost to have
been supernaturally deposited into the genes, as I
implied earlier. If it is properly enhanced by both people and
circumstance, it will blossom at just the right moment.
That certainly was true of Joseph.

Charlie Brower, an industrialist, has said, "Few people
are successful unless a lot of other people want them to
be." Enlarging upon Brower's observation, it could be
argued that few leaders with a sense of destiny ever obtain a
position of leadership unless others want them to.
Therefore, it is a miracle that Joseph survived. Are there
would-be leaders in our time that have not survived? Are
there leaders who were prematurely set aside, squelched,

picked over because we gave them no room to grow?

The supreme test of Joseph's sense of destiny came first when he found himself at the bottom of a pit selected by his enraged brothers. One has to believe that there were some terrifying moments when Joseph lay at the bottom of that empty cistern looking upward at the opening into the faces of his older brothers. What thought coursed through the young man's mind as he faced the full fury of their rejection? He must have known that the majority of them wanted to murder him at that moment and were restrained only by the courageous Reuben. Did he at any time slip into self-doubt? Did it ever occur to him to ask if one could not convince his own family could he convince anyone else?

Is it not the ultimate in rejection when one's own family fails to recognize and affirm one's sense of being? Joseph would not have needed psychological terms to face all this. Even if there were no terms to describe them in his times, the feelings were just as real and their effects just as potentially devastating. His resilience in the face of such a crisis is a certain evidence that the foundations of leadership were already set in place.

Another point worth noting about Joseph in his boyhood was that he was always seen in a serving posture. His boyhood reports about his brothers were an effort to serve his father's best interests. He seemed to have understood responsibility and accountability, and he was always uneasy when things were upset. He willed right things for his father, the man in charge.

Looking ahead in Joseph's life in the house of Potiphar, he marshalled his destiny to the best interests of the owner of that household. Again he served the captain of the guard, the head of the jail when he became a prisoner. No wonder he was ready to serve Pharaoh. In all four cases Joseph gave no sign of seeking the number one position. Rather he sought only the best interests of the person in charge. He wanted what was best for everyone involved. Again, those instincts are a sense of destiny at work in its purest form.

These general overviews of Joseph's younger years are simply descriptions of the raw material which was slowly being processed into a man "in whom is the spirit of God." Years later the job of leadership in Egypt would require not only people marked with an intellectual and managerial brilliance, but people whose quality of spirit would make them capable of leading others to respond also on the level of the inner spirit. The Egyptian austerity programs would require not only conformity to whatever laws Joseph might pass, but they would demand that people obey with enthusiasm. It meant that people would be compelled to say no to their natural instincts and swing to spiritual qualities of life such as restraint and discipline. Again, to get people to do that would require of a leader enormous spiritual charisma. The charisma was in the process of development back in Joseph's boyhood.

After analyzing the accounts of Joseph's boyhood, I am no longer surprised when I reflect upon the episodes the writer chose to describe Joseph's upbringing. The writer was trying to show the reader the continuity between Joseph the boy and Joseph the leader. Perhaps that is why the biography of Joseph touches also upon another crisis in early adult years when Joseph's moral integrity could be spotlighted and explained.

Potiphar, his estate and his wife—that was to be the theater in which another great quality of the young leader's life would be tested and proven. Brought to Egypt as a slave, Joseph epitomized the ironies of God in history. He who arrives as a slave will leave later as a king. Does it portend the way of the Christ who will come in weakness as a babe, die an apparent criminal, rise in power, ascend in glory, reign as Son, and come again as King?

Joseph's excellence as an administrator emerged under Potiphar. The time span is hazy; the exact details sparse. But the writer is explicit enough to tell us that within a short period of years, Joseph was controlling Potiphar's entire business empire. That destiny, from a heavenly perspective, was riding on Joseph's shoulders is indicated by the writer of Genesis when he says:

The Lord was with Joseph, and he became a successful man . . . and his master saw that the Lord was with him, and that the Lord caused all that he did to prosper in his hands. So Joseph found favor in his sight and attended him, and he made him overseer of his house and put him in charge of all that he had. [Gen. 39:2-4]

One cannot escape the additional irony that Potiphar, a pagan businessman, saw qualities and abilities in Joseph that his own family had failed to see. That insight again needs to be enlarged with the comment that our human condition often causes us to be blind to the gifts and potentials of our closest friends and relatives. More than one leader has had to fight his best friends to become himself and realize his potential. The same is true for the poet, the artist, the composer. It is no wonder that Rollo May once commented that the creative person's worst enemies are often his or her best friends.

The author of Genesis seems to be pointing out Potiphar's shrewdness. He was ready to climb aboard the momentum developed by a man blessed of God. Too bad Joseph's father and brothers weren't as smart as Potiphar. Perhaps they would have profited by Joseph's ability. Potiphar saw what they chose to be blind to. It wasn't as if Joseph hadn't given his father and his brothers a chance to see the same brilliance that Potiphar later spotted.

The crises at Potiphar's house would have been the ruin of most men. It wasn't for Joseph because he knew his limits: administratively, relationally, and morally. Joseph knew what he was in charge of, *and* he knew what he wasn't in charge of. Leaders know limits, and Joseph knew that the limit of his virtually unlimited control of Potiphar's interests stopped at the boss's wife.

Put bluntly, Joseph was propositioned. Given the choice of words with which the writer describes the proposition placed before Joseph by Potiphar's wife, it was plainly a cheap, thrill-oriented affair that she suggested. She was attracted by his good looks, and beyond that, his apparent charisma. Joseph's qualities drew first Potiphar to use him for business purposes and then Potiphar's wife to propose the use of him for immoral purposes. There is nothing unusual about that.

From the outset of this difficult experience, Joseph understood the motives of these two people and what his response should be. He had no trouble agreeing to Potiphar's plan for his life; but he was not about to be taken in by Potiphar's wife. He saw through seductive compliments and flirtatious expressions. In short, he knew when he was being appreciated for the right qualities. That alone shows emerging conviction and self-awareness. This ability to discern between appropriate compliments and affirmations and those which are destructive has often been a dividing point between those who went on to greatness and those who remained behind as moral and spiritual casualties.

The significance of the temptation experience between Joseph and Potiphar's wife lies not only in that it happened but in its frequency. These words "lie with me," an invitation to a brief interlude of sexual pleasure came not once or twice, but "every day." The writer is talking about an indeterminate time period during which a number of things could and probably did happen.

For one thing a frequent, almost rhythmic, temptation must have begun to burrow its way down to the depths of Joseph's mind, his emotions, and his natural instincts. We do Joseph a serious injustice if we think that he was automatically impervious to this temptation. The fact that she came to him every day is evidence that Potiphar's wife thought him "reachable." Only after a long while did the matter reach a crescendo in which Joseph violently rejected her.

It could also be surmised that the woman's approaches became increasingly overt and bold. She obviously was a deceitful person whose ardor would measurably increase as the "forbidden fruit" failed to fall into her hands. The more Joseph resisted, the more imaginative she probably became.

I think we are being fair to Joseph if we suggest that during that time when the temptation came with insistence, he wrestled with enormous thoughts during which his entire future hung in the balance. We have to believe that there was a part of Joseph that would have

liked to give in. Not to believe that would be to suggest that
Joseph was incapable of sin. Even that driving sense of
destiny forming within him could have gotten out of hand
in such a time as this, causing him to want to possess
everything in his path. Destiny could have become blind
ambition, insisting that his mind reason with words such
as, "I have everything else in Potiphar's house, why not his
wife?" Or, "I'm big enough to handle everything else; I
can handle this too!" Certainly he could have concluded
that he deserved what Potiphar's wife offered. Is this not a
personal sort of turbulence which anyone must face sooner
or later?

Being isolated from supportive relationships, being a
young man with all the physical and emotional drives and
needs—perhaps even deep-seated feelings of bitterness
against a system which forced him into slavery—could
have all conspired to cause him to weaken to the
temptation. Joseph had every human excuse, including
the alibi that it was her idea, and who was he to say no.

Yet he said no. "How can I do this great wickedness
and sin against God?" Here is the key to Joseph's growing
sense of integrity. He equated sin against his boss as sin
against God. To hurt one was to hurt the other. From that
equation comes integrity.

What might have happened if he had given in? And add to
that hypothesis the possibility that having given in he
would have gotten away with it.

Such a strain on his integrity would have denied him
the moral and spiritual fiber he would need later as ruler in
Egypt. If the seductions of a beautiful woman had reached
the will of Joseph, he would have been a "sitting duck" for
those far more expert in the art of bribe when he reached
a higher position of power. We have to assume that Joseph,
when he was later in power, was approached constantly by
Egyptians offering virtually everything in the way of favors
if he would make exceptions, provide preferential
treatment, or look the other way at key moments when laws
needed to be subverted or suspended for someone's
convenience.

That he could later maintain an impeccable record

during fourteen stressful years has to be traced back to his ability to develop such a record in the house of Potiphar. And Potiphar's wife was the greatest test in earlier years to see if he had what it took to make it in later years.

The past years of American history have seen an almost endless parade of political and industrial leadership facing prosecution for charges spanning from bribery and corruption to sex scandals. Cover-ups, kickbacks, and stonewalling are familiar terms to us all. They are a large part of the reason that few Americans trust anyone in government today. Few leaders have actually been able to convince the American public that their word is their bond. That Joseph would never have such a problem is revealed already in his successful confrontation of the crisis with Potiphar's wife.

Joseph's commitment to Potiphar, to God, and to his own integrity landed him in jail. It's been pointed out many times that his sentence to jail is probably a quiet admission on Potiphar's part that he never believed the claim of rape that his wife made against Joseph. If she had been credible, there would have been airtight grounds for Joseph's immediate execution. That he went to jail and not to the gallows may be a sorrowful admission by Potiphar that he knew his wife was lying. But in order to save face and maintain the family reputation, Potiphar was forced to turn against Joseph rather than publicly dishonor his wife. Perhaps it was Potiphar's loyalty and appreciation for Joseph that made him settle for prison rather than a charade of vindictiveness which would have brought on Joseph's execution.

This encounter between Joseph and Potiphar's family which ended in tragedy also tells us something about Joseph's perspective on labor. His integrity was not only revealed in the sexual and relational sense but it was also reflected in terms of his view of work. It is obvious that Joseph saw that serving God and serving a boss are much the same matter, demanding the same performance and attitude. Service to one is service to the other.

Howard Hendricks tells of meeting an airline flight attendant who performed admirably during a stressful

series of encounters with a disgruntled passenger. When the
flight had ended Dr. Hendricks went to her and affirmed
her for her gracious spirit and requested her name and
employee number so that he could write to the airline
and convey a commendation. Her response was "Sir, I don't
work for _____ _____ airlines: I work for Jesus Christ."
That may be one key to integrity: it worked for her, and it
worked for Joseph.

Once again we continue with the question: What qualities
and background experiences develop a man like Joseph?
Again, the writer has told us little, but what he has
indicated seems clearly significant. He has informed us
that Joseph had a sense of destiny, that he possessed
enormous integrity and loyalty. I think I hear him telling
us at least one more thing.

Call it *excellence*. It is a standard by which one does
things, a standard of personhood. It means doing and being
all things to the very best possible limit. This quality in
Joseph's life probably impresses the reader more during the
prison sequence of Joseph's experiences than at any other
time. Why, after rejection from family and false
representation at Potiphar's house, does this man choose
a third time to support the people in charge of a system?
What is it that compels a man to accept the adverse
circumstances, without bitterness and vindictiveness, and
to get on with the business of insuring that even a prison
will be run efficiently and effectively?

It is not hard to imagine Joseph being brought to
prison. Was there a brief orientation period in those days as
there is today? Was there some Egyptian counterpart to
being fingerprinted, issued prison clothes, interviewed by
the deputy warden, and assigned a job within the prison
system? Did Joseph face a short period of culture shock as he
adjusted to a prisoner's way of life? And then did he begin
to look around and begin to see that things in this prison
could be a lot better if someone applied himself to getting
things done? Early in his prison stay it became plain that
Joseph wasn't going to sit around. As a prisoner Joseph
could choose between excellence or mediocrity. He chose
the former; it was his nature.

Is mediocrity a characteristic of life and work that usually marks most human beings? Nicholas Murray Butler, former president of Columbia University, was thinking in this direction when he wrote, "I classify the people of the world in three categories: the few who *make* things happen; the many who *watch* things happen; and the overwhelming majority *who have no idea* of what is happening."

People who make things happen usually make them happen excellently, wherever they are: in a capitol building, in a pulpit, on a construction project, in a surgical theater, in an artist's studio, and even—strangely enough—in a prison. Where there is excellence, there is outstanding achievement. Where there is such achievement, all are blest; all profit.

One would think it is a long way from a prison compound to a palace audience with the pharaoh of Egypt. It would seem, however, the prison was only an anteroom to Pharaoh's court where Joseph waited until God was ready to orchestrate their encounter. The two men and the crises they would meet together were only a short distance apart. Yet even then, there was plenty of opportunity for Joseph to adopt what must have been a prevailing philosophy in prison: quit, grow bitter, serve aimless time.

But the decision for excellence in prison performance by the young son of Jacob made that jail merely a finishing school. Under the extreme duress of that grimy place, Joseph simply worked at perfecting the skills he had once dreamed of utilizing while he slept out among the hills of his homeland. How curious that God would use a prison to do his finishing work on a man soon to lead a large nation. But then why should we be surprised? God has used deserts, alien countries, and carpentry shops to sculpture his special people before and after Joseph.

What God seeks are not the degrees and the highly specialized criteria that often accredit people today to a professional elite. Rather, he sought then and seeks today men and women willing to undergo the stress training that makes them capable of developing integrity, destiny, and excellence so that they can walk among earth's noises and hear the whispers of God.

That Joseph finally stands at the end of a long journey before Pharaoh is no accident or coincidence. It is simply the opening act of a drama symbolized in boyhood dreams. It is not a moment pursued by ambition but by careful, deliberate living according to the laws of God. And now that the young man is there in the palace, he acts calmly, with certitude. He is not intimidated; he is not indecisive; he shows no sign that he needs this big moment to be anything more than he already is. Joseph has performed before in his father's business; he has performed in Potiphar's house; he has performed in prison. While the implications of this moment may be greater in scale, the standards and qualities by which he will act are simply the same as on earlier occasions.

Years after the moment of Pharaoh's choice, Joseph reached that climactic moment when he was reunited with his family. The dreams did indeed come true: there was much bowing and adulation. Joseph's response to the reappearance of his family showed other qualities that had grown within his inner spirit. One was that he was not vindictive. Rather than use his newly acquired power to gain revenge over his brothers who had made his childhood years miserable, he chose to forgive and redeem.

But perhaps the most remarkable insight of all is Joseph's awareness that a living God had been in charge of this incredible chain of events from the very beginning. Speaking to his brothers Joseph commented, "The things you did to me, you meant for evil; but God meant them for good that many might be saved in this day."

It is difficult to avoid the question: Where are the "Josephs" today? But there is no use asking such a question unless we deal with its counterpart: Are people willing to follow a Joseph should he appear? And a third query: Are there many who think in terms of creating the circumstances in which "Josephs" are born and prepared? Hard questions; hard answers. But these are turbulent days, and in the eighties and nineties the turbulence will increase.

AXIOM TWO
A person for turbulent times nurtures a resilient faith—not the sort that causes one to retreat from the world, but a faith which compels him or her to permeate the world with a formidable healing and redeeming energy.

4/ A slow-motion replay

Can you perceive why my fascination with Joseph has remained undiminished for years? He was a childhood hero, and he was a teenage model. Today he is an adult inspiration. I have found him to be an extraordinary contemporary personality, by no means a dusty ancient.

I have a name for the quality this young man possessed that provided him with the credentials to stand as God's man in Egypt—*authentic charisma.* Since the word charisma is so thoroughly overused and misunderstood, I shall qualify it with the adjective, authentic.

Assess for a moment what this man with authentic charisma accomplished: (1) he convinced the leaders of a great nation of his own credibility even though he came straight from a prison; (2) he stepped into a "wisdom gap" providing answers to people who didn't even know the questions; (3) he identified a pending crisis and the proper response to it; (4) he showed himself to be the only viable candidate for bringing the strategy for survival to a successful completion; (5) he made the strategy work.

Joseph's accomplishments in Egypt become more impressive when one recalls that he became the top man in a culture which had no knowledge of or sympathy with his God. As far as we can determine, he stood alone in his convictions. There was no one around to offer him fellowship or affirmation. His spiritual resources appear to have come exclusively from heaven.

The prime issues in Egypt were not economic; they were spiritual. Thus it took a man with a conditional spirit to see beneath the surface and expose those issues. Could the Egyptian people be challenged and organized to resist the instincts of selfishness and intemperance in order to face a serious food shortage and survive? *Only* if there was the influence of authentic charisma among them.

I am greatly impressed with the similarities between Joseph's era in Egypt and our turbulent times. They both share the problem of pending crises, of confused leadership, of finding a new and improved life-style which demands strengthened spiritual roots. What they do not share in similarity is the fact that Egypt was impacted by a Joseph; our age has not been marked by a man like that yet.

All of my efforts to interpret Joseph's life for our age will be betrayed, however, if I convey the idea that we should seek a single leader to ascend to high political places and miraculously lead millions of people away from spiritual disaster. It could happen of course, but such is not my main concern.

I am much more content if the story of Joseph could cause a few common Christians like myself to become acquainted with the Joseph-style of authentic charisma, for the principle of his life must be pressed into service at every level of our society. "Josephs" make effective fathers (and mothers); "Josephs" make good pastors, good student leaders, good business people, good thinkers. Our age does not need *a* Joseph as much as it needs a plethora of "Josephs," living his theme of authentic charisma before large and small groups of people.

I am a Christian pastor committed irrevocably to the genius of the congregation and the family as centers for

immense spiritual influence within a world. I do not wish
to be disloyal or seem unaffectionate toward my own
Christian loyalties when I comment that Joseph-like
charisma hardly exists today. I grow troubled when I learn
that Christian church membership is reputed to be at an
all-time high in the United States, and yet Christian
influence is perhaps at an all-time low. I am perplexed at
surveys that report the number of people professing some
sort of personal relationship with Christ to be between
thirty and forty million; yet Christian influence seems
hardly existent in our age. It is a bothersome thought that
general Christian influence was greatest in our nation
during times when church attendance was proportionately
much less than it is today.

The reader has to understand that influence—
authentic charisma—is not evidenced by the fact that
Christian preaching and personalities enjoy high exposure
on mass media. Nor is it influenced if many national
luminaries profess to have had a born-again experience.

Christian influence or authentic charisma exists if
there is a measurable fear or respect when a Christian
speaks on issues of life. When there is a hunger by
society to know what the Christian position is on any
particular issue. When what the Christian thinks is
wrong is quickly addressed by those in power and brought
to some sort of solution.

Apart from a few valiant efforts on the part of certain
individuals, it cannot be said that direct Christian
influence has played a part in bringing the races closer,
solving the problems of our cities, shortening the agonies
of Vietnam or Watergate, shedding light on the human rights
problem around the world, sharpening the conscience of
America on matters such as consumption of food, energy,
or other raw materials. The Christian community, not
having said much on these issues, does not seem likely to
have much to say on future issues of much greater import.
We simply have no agenda that speaks to the affairs of our
troubled age.

The Jewish humorist, Harry Golden, said: "If I were faced
with the decision today to join a Christian church or die, I

would not hesitate for a minute to join. There's nothing to offend me in the modern church." I'm not saying we ought to think of something that will successfully offend Harry Golden, but I do ask if his assessment of the level of contemporary Christian commitment is worth considering. Is the Christian community that impotent? The gospel of Christ certainly isn't.

What have we done that we have become so widely ignored? Joseph had a message that spoke to the issue of *his time*. The Christian has a message that begins with the power of Jesus Christ to change a person's life and bring him into relationship with God. But the message does not stop there. A person is redeemed to be a Joseph in his age. Having been made ready, he or she must become responsible. Responsibility, I suggest, means getting out of the canoe and fighting the pollution.

The football coach, the sales manager, and the laboratory technician often use video tapes to reexamine crucial plays, product presentations, and key experiments. I want to replay the Joseph story again and again in the pursuit of what it means to bring authentic charisma to bear within a crisis-oriented age. I want to thrust a zoom lens back and forth across the life of the young man of Egypt in order to find out what made him as effective in his world as he obviously was. Be patient with me if, like a coach, I stop the projector and review the same moment several times. Permit me license to suggest what might be lurking between the lines of the story.

There is only one serious risk in a search for the sources of Joseph's authentic charisma and that is the possibility that, should one uncover useful answers, he or she might find them frighteningly intimidating. That has already been my own experience. There have been many private moments when I felt that I was handling a quantity of spiritual nitroglycerin. The reader may discover, as I have, that getting too close to Joseph becomes an explosive experience, presenting rebukes so strong and challenges so great that it becomes difficult to live peaceably with spiritual mediocrity ever again.

AXIOM THREE
**A person for turbulent times understands that the primary
struggles of any generation are spiritual in nature and that the
solutions are found in a man's or woman's submission to God.
Although such a person is knowledgeable about the world's
problems his or her primary concern centers on the cleansing of
the spirit and the search for truth.**

5/ The pursuit of authentic charisma

Wherever Joseph went, he forced people to face some
dimension of reality and respond to it. That is important! It
happened within the stifling embrace of his small-
thinking family; it occurred in the prosperous offices and
fields of an Egyptian estate; and it happened again during
his unjust confinement among the prisoners who
comprised the desperate and dismal community of a
military jail. In each case both the high and the lowly were
confronted with truth about their past behavior, or their
present performance, or even their future potential.

Watch Joseph! His effect upon people seems to have
been very consistent. No one was ever left the same. With
him around, people and events always changed. What was
it? What quality within his character and personality made
him climb to the top in people's esteem?

I'm drawn to the word *charisma*, meaning "gifted," a label
which describes a person who draws people and realities
together and causes things to happen.

I think I can almost hear the reader groan inwardly at the word charisma—first, because of its overuse within our age, and, second, because of its unfortunate application to all sorts of people who have gained fame for achievements not always consonant with our understanding of Scripture.

But I propose that we seize the word back; it comes from too good a verbal heritage to surrender it now. Should we choose to examine its classical meaning, we might discover that it once again fits the dimensions of a Joseph and also the kind of leadership we seek in the last turbulent decades of the twentieth century. Should we agree to search for its more accurate meaning, among the very first things to go would be the contemporary concept that charisma means glamour or "macho," a word used in the American culture to describe sensual masculinity.

We would also probably agree that charisma should not describe—in its purest sense—that which is the biggest or the most beautiful. Nor would it correctly mark the communicator whose capability is more in communication than in the development of content. Today many of those called charismatic by their contemporaries have their speeches or their monologues written for them by other professionals. Strange!

Again, charisma should not rightly describe slickness, or speed, or even persuasive abilities that cause people to be led against their own best interests to do the will of the persuader.

Charisma is not an appropriate word to describe the person who makes a living by appealing to the emotions of people, or to their baser instincts. And charisma should not be definitive of the person who discerns from polls and surveys what people want to hear and then tells it to them. One is struck by recent experiments in which political scientists have conducted surveys of the opinions of people, fed the results into a computer programmed to construct a speech using the collected data. When a speaker read the computer-written speech, he was greeted with a standing ovation.

Charisma ought not to mean—as many think it does—sheer popularity, assigned by mobs of people usually more interested in escape *from* than in confrontation *with* reality. All of this—and much more—needs to be stripped away from the word charisma in order to uncover its true meaning, reaching toward something which more aptly describes Joseph of Egypt and not the "beautiful people" of a troubled age.

Charisma is not a quality possessed only by heads of government, or championship athletes, or to crowd-pleasing entertainers. Once understood, charisma, we shall all find, denotes a quality of leadership and authority that ought to be found in homes, neighborhoods, congregations and in any place where people converge for mutual cooperation and support.

The Greek word *charisma* was used to picture someone gifted by the gods. A gifted person! Special. Capable. Worth watching and following. Joseph was a man gifted by Jehovah, his God, from the very start, and he was gifted to shape the circumstances of his times. He was there to introduce order into chaos, to thrust illumination into darkness. He did it because he was gifted.

What set Joseph apart from others in terms of his charisma was something spiritual in quality and impact. The biographer of Joseph spends much more time describing Joseph's spiritual makeup than his abilities or skills.

"The Lord was with Joseph, and he became a successful man," the writer says. The writer believed the key to Joseph's success was the intimate relationship between Joseph and his God.

The nature of authentic charisma is a quality of character in personhood which is far deeper and more insightful than human skills or an enthusiasm which ellicits only temporary emotional response.

Nowhere have I seen this fact better illustrated than in Langdon Gilkey's book *The Shantung Compound* (New York: Harper and Row, 1975). Gilkey wrote of 2,000 Western people with whom he was interned by the Japanese army for two years in a small hospital complex in northern China during World War II. Placed under close guard, they were told by the Japanese commandant that they would have to develop and maintain their own community structures for the purposes of allocating what living space, food, and heating fuel would be rationed to them. Needless to say, everything was in short supply, and there was almost immediate tension between the British, Dutch, South African, and American men and women in the Shantung Compound.

"At this point [the very beginning of the internment]. . . we were an uncoordinated mass of humanity," Gilkey recalled. "We had to tackle together certain basic problems if we were merely to survive. Such a community needed organized leadership as much as it needed anything."

Gilkey's account of the formulation of leadership within the community is fascinating. As a young liberal optimist, the author recounted his own delight in the early days at Shantung as he took stock of the enormous human resources available among the internees. There were engineers to solve the problems of shelter, managers to coordinate the distribution of food and clothing, diplomats and politicians to create structures of relationship and policy, business leaders to solve problems, teachers to teach, artists to entertain. Everyone, Gilkey wrote, had a purpose that would be integral to the needs and ultimate survival of the internees.

I think I hear Gilkey at the outset of the book almost reveling in the opportunity to observe firsthand the ideal conditions under which human beings could work together and create the perfect community, something which would bring out the best in everyone. Everyone had a useful purpose, he went on to observe; everyone *except*, in his initial opinion, the preacher and the missionary. People with experience in preaching and theologizing seemed obsolete, irrelevant, and purposeless in this community of the skilled, in this place where the best in everyone should be brought to the surface. At least that is what Gilkey thought.

It didn't take long for Langdon Gilkey to discover that life at Shantung Compound was not going to live up to his enthusiastic expectations. Into the system created by the most highly skilled of organizers, managers, and tacticians, there began to creep a kind of spiritual cancer that permeated almost every level of relationship. No one was immune, it seemed, from the petty squabbles that soon broke out over all sorts of issues.

There was stealing from the kitchen by those who felt they deserved more food than the daily ration allowed. Chunks of coal were taken from the storage lockers by those in charge of fuel distribution. Those responsible for space allocation granted themselves a few extra square feet of sleeping room that they normally assigned to others. Some responsible for the maintenance of the latrines resented the humbling nature of their task and performed poorly. A few with political skill repeatedly misused it. The "best" Gilkey expected became the "worst."

By the midpoint of Gilkey's account of events at Shantung, he was admittedly a discouraged man. What had he learned? That skill by itself is an inadequate resource for the creation and maintenance of a healthy community. What was necessary, Gilkey painfully began to discover for himself, was someone who could speak to the spirits of people, giving them cause and purpose for the direction of their skills. Until there was an underlying foundation that would bolster attitudes, engender self-restraint, and cause people to seek the advancement of the interests and needs of others, nothing was going to happen except continuing deterioration of morale and living conditions. Indeed it became necessary for the captives of Shantung to appeal to the Japanese commandant to settle some of their disputes. Where grace cannot be brought to bear, law must apparently abound.

Reading Gilkey's account of the deterioration of the Shantung community must be done with the memory of his earlier observation that the preachers of Shantung were possessors of what he thought to be irrelevant skills. Perhaps his evaluation was forerunner to the present tendency of many in our society who use words like "preacher" or "preachy" to put down anyone who appeals to moral and spiritual sensitivities.

When the President of the United States earnestly appealed to the American people to carefully curtail their needless use of scarce energy and called for unity of spirit, mutual cooperation, renewed belief in enduring ideals, what was the reaction of his opponents? They responded by calling his speech a "sermon" and him a "preacher." In so doing, they tell us something about contemporary attitudes. We are a people who do not want to be preached at. We say that we've been told what to do, pushed around, one too many times. Let us think for ourselves, we say. "So don't preach," we tell anyone who speaks to us on the level of the "ought" or the "should."

By such reactions we admit that preaching implies a content of information or challenge which comes not from opinion surveys or polls, not from experiments in a laboratory, and not from the wellspring of the entertainer's mind. But rather we sense that preaching implies content that comes from a possible higher source and does not need to be footnoted or documented. Preaching appeals to deeper and immeasurable value systems; it comes from models of character out of the past which rebuke us to the bone. We don't like to face such content because it's difficult to refute, so we ridicule it and we call anyone who appeals to these spiritual resources a preacher and what he or she says is preaching. And preaching is generally dismissed, as it was at Shantung, as irrelevant.

The longer Langdon Gilkey watched the slow deterioration of things at Shantung, the more obliged he was to admit that there was a need for some sort of preaching. If only someone could have come along who would have won the ears and hearts of the internees and convinced them of the spiritual pollution and the need to stop their graft, their stealing, the needless conflict, the insatiable greed! Apparently what he longed for was not the skills of the politician, the manager, the engineer, or the businessman. For that, one needs a preacher, and, unfortunately, the few professional preachers that were at Shantung were not strong enough to do the job.

But perhaps the major point worth observing is Gilkey's subtle admission that the preacher might have potentially been the most important person at Shantung. If there had only been someone there with authentic charisma. But there wasn't and the whole community suffered.

The Shantung Compound is a magnificent though dismal parable of the world community. As did Gilkey, any observer of our age would quickly affirm that our society does not lack for skills in all the sciences, in technology, in politics, in the arts, in the worlds of education, the military, even theology. And as it seemed to Gilkey, it appears that an underlying theme of our age has been the universal assumption that accumulated knowledge and ability will bring every human problem under control, every conflict to peaceful solution. And to be fair and honest, one must admit that measurable strides forward have been taken in many areas of life. But it is just as fair to say that the spirit of humanity still remains dangerously savage.

Our countryside is perforated with missile silos; many streets of our cities are hardly safer than a battleground; the courts in which contracts of marriage, business, and responsibility are evaluated are jammed to capacity by those seeking to break them. Our skills have tamed everything but ourselves.

Once again, this is where the search for authentic charisma begins. Or perhaps our civilization has made the same wrong assumption that Langdon Gilkey started with when he arrived at Shantung. For it is not at the level of skill that problems are started on their way to solution. Rather it is the level of the inner human spirit which must be reached—the place where one nurses commitments and convictions, where one hears the whispers of God, where one makes moral determinations. Here it is that we should have made our leaps of progress forward. Since our priorities have not been spiritual we are a weakening people, and it is reasonable to fear collapse in the face of the

turbulence which approaches us in the eighties and
nineties. It was a collapse that faced Egypt thousands of
years ago, and at that time they were graced by God with
a person of authentic charisma.

I hear John Gardner musing upon this theme of concern
when he writes:

The renewal of societies and organizations can go forward
only if someone cares. Apathy and lowered motivation are
the most widely noted characteristics of a civilization on
the downward path. Apathetic men accomplish nothing.
Men who believe in nothing change nothing for the better.
They renew nothing and heal no one, least of all
themselves. Anyone who understands our situation at all
knows that we are in little danger of failing through lack
of material strength. *If we falter, it will be a failure of heart
and spirit* (italics mine). [*Self Renewal* (New York:
Perennial, Harper and Row, 1963)]

The question that faced Egypt at that time is the same one
that faces us today at every level of human relationship.
"Where can we find the persons in whom are the spirits of
the gods?" In other words, where are the people with
authentic charisma?

It is thought-provoking that, in an advanced society
such as Egypt, the pharaoh could not find the kind of man
with the charisma needed for the crisis that was foretold
in his dream. It is ironic that a pagan ruler had to reach
outside his society to save it. That he ultimately turned
to Joseph is not only a comment about Joseph; it is an
indictment of Egypt. It too was a society rich in skills,
but apparently impoverished in spirit. There was no
Egyptian who had the spiritual authority necessary to
guide and direct the Egyptian people and give shape to their
turbulent times.

Thus Joseph was the fresh new breath of air. He was God's
man when the pharaoh's man didn't exist. A frightening
parallel to our times.

The plea for a special kind of Joseph leadership had
reached upward toward the level of a collective scream

within our Western society. We would hardly attach
significance to a dream today, but indeed the same message
that sprang from Pharaoh's dream comes to us today
from different kinds of sources. Computers, highly
sophisticated systems of measurement and
prognostication, scholars, and researchers seem to be
communicating a theme which offers little to cheer
about. Their concerted cry boils down to the message
"Turbulence!" Who will lead us through?

I am reminded of the story that has been frequently told
of the Titanic as it streamed through the North Atlantic
Ocean on its collision course with disaster. Radio reports
kept coming to the wireless operator in the Titanic's
communication center telling of dangerous icebergs ahead.
But the technician's reaction was to ask the sender to
cease jamming the airwaves so that it would be easier for
the Titanic's officers to get the results of a famous race back
in England.

Somehow the bearer of the message was unable to
communicate an adequate warning to the self-confident
ship. And because both speaker and listener failed in that
endeavor, the Titanic went to the bottom of the sea, a
fitting allegory for many past and present civilizations.

Senator Mark Hatfield writes:

From my perspective there has never been a greater
demand for positive, creative, committed leadership—at
every level, in every area—than today. We need a leadership
that dominates change rather than one that merely reacts
to it. We need a leadership with broad knowledge, great
vision, *and a commitment to serving the needs of others
rather than one that feeds on opportunities for personal
gain* (italics mine). [*Conflict and Conscience* (Waco TX:
Word, 1971)]

Perhaps it is time to remind ourselves that we are
reshaping the word charisma, giving it a restored meaning
which means we are moving it from the dimension of the
skilled or the emotional to the dimension of the
spiritual. My purpose is the deliberate redeployment of the

word. It is folly to speak of future survival and the advancement of the human experience if we do not reach the heart through people whose hearts are already reached.

Again, what Joseph did for Egypt was far more spiritual than logistical or managerial. While he did manage the nation through crises, it was only because he first brought himself and then the nation to deal with the spiritual realities of the day. If he had not convinced the Egyptians of the necessity of restraining themselves during the seven years of plenty, he would have had no relief program to manage during the seven years of want and famine.

What we seek does not always imply success with all human beings who are affected. Authentic charisma tends to polarize people about vital issues. It forces them to either align themselves with the standards of rightness and righteousness implied in the issue, or it demands of them that they stand up and be counted in their rejection of whatever they are called upon to be or to do. Authentic charisma permits no listener to be neutral.

The most perfect model of charisma would have to be of course Jesus Christ. How frequently students of Christ have observed that no one ever left his presence morally or spiritually neutral over what he was or said. His charisma directed people to an acceptance of his lordship, or it surfaced their antipathies and made them choose to become outraged enemies.

This sort of polarization happened wherever Joseph entered into relationships. His charisma polarized his brothers; it drew Potiphar; it attracted the captain of the guard at the prison. It just may have frightened the pharaoh's butler—Joseph's old prisonmate—who seems to have conveniently "forgotten" Joseph—perhaps out of fear, or because he saw Joseph as a threat to himself or what he stood for.

Joseph's charisma certainly had an effect upon Potiphar's wife. She seems to symbolize what happened to Jesus in the early days of his ministry in the wilderness. The Adversary attempted to sidetrack Christ and seduce him to interests not in line with his basic purpose for coming to earth. Both Joseph and Jesus, by their charisma, first attracted the enemy and then, when it became obvious that they could not be bought, repelled the enemy.

We must avoid this trap of equating what we are calling charisma with the idea that it is irresistibly attractive to everyone. A far clearer understanding would be to suggest that authentic charisma forces everyone in its presence to become honest with themselves, with God, and with the issues.

It should begin to become plain why one might have authentic charisma and yet be classified by the culture as a failure. What might one have said, for example, of John the Baptist soon after his beheading? Or of Jesus soon after his crucifixion? Or of Paul soon after his execution? In the short-term view, their charisma seems to have been a failure. Not so! In the long-term we know that their charisma was authentic. They were indeed gifted by God, and their charisma did indeed force those about them to change. Beware, therefore, of those who measure the authenticity of true charisma with the age's view of success.

James MacGregor Burns recalls an oft-related story about a Frenchman sitting in a cafe who suddenly hears a disturbance outside. He jumps to his feet and cries "There goes the mob! I am their leader! I must follow them!"

Such is the illustration of what authentic charisma— being gifted by the gods—is not. The eighties and nineties must not seek leadership which is gifted by either the aged self or the mob; rather it must seek him or her gifted from a Source much greater than and beyond all of us, a Source which knows the end from the beginning because it has created the end and the beginning. Those who walk among us with gifts from that God will perform great service for families, for communities, for churches, for nations. They will bring order out of chaos; flush falsehood from truth; give strength to what is weak.

A friend of many years comes periodically to visit my wife and me in our home. He is the head of a Christian organization whose personnel are scattered throughout the Caribbean and into southern Europe. His mind is necessarily filled with a thousand details: administrative decisions, fund-raising, and what he will have to preach about at the next church he visits, a problem needing solution, his own mental and physical fatigue. But when he comes—often very tired—to our home, he brings with him something of a breath of spiritual fresh air. He sits with my wife and me at our supper table late into the evening and speaks of God, insights from Scripture, applications to real life. And when we retire to our beds exhausted from the long hours of conversation, we are refreshed in our spirits. The issues of our lives have been reprioritized. We have come face to face with the living God again. We are reenergized to the acts of servanthood and witness. With his presence and personhood he has brought all of that to us, and he has brought it out of us. He has authentic charisma, and he does for us what Joseph did for Egypt.

Joseph has been dead for over 4,000 years. Is it pure sentimentality that one wishes for his rebirth? Or does Joseph simply possess ageless qualities that will fit any generation, qualities which when unleashed might yet bring joy to a future age which is rapidly dwindling into glumness.

No, I'll not ask for Joseph. Rather I'll ask for men and women like him, persons fit for turbulent times, like our Lord, like my friend who comes periodically to visit, and I'll ask that the authentic charisma also be a part of my own life. Perhaps one by one we can enlarge the swell and redeem our own Egypt.

AXIOM FOUR
A person for turbulent times appreciates the fact that time, pressure, pain, submission, and even failure are among God's primary tools used to mold people. Knowing this, he or she sees the opportunity for growth in every obstacle and finds possibility for maturity in every problem.

6/ The elements of authentic charisma

Again and again my "projector" replays the story of Joseph's life, and each time I look for those special keys which may have been too obvious or too obscure to see at first glance. What are those elements which caused Jacob's eleventh son to move on to the stage of Egyptian history and bring a mighty nation under his leadership?

Two analogies out of modern experience assist me in the search. A friend shares with me, for example, the story of a tourist who entered a mountain gift shop in the deep South and became immediately impressed with a vast display of carved wooden figures of various breeds of dogs. The lifelikeness of each of the carvings on the shelf was so remarkable that the tourist could not resist asking the clerk where the carver could be found. A finger pointed toward a back room to which the curious traveler headed.

The tourist found the carver of the dogs in the back of the shop, sitting amidst a pile of woodchips, making swift, sure cuts with a sharp knife in a block of wood that was already beginning to take the shape of still another

dog. After a period of respectful silence in which the
tourist watched in fascination, he asked, "What is the
secret of such wonderful work?"

The response was simple, quick, and left little room for
a follow-up question. The woodcarver quietly drawled, "I
just take a block of good wood, and I cut away everything
that obviously isn't a dog."

The Joseph that stood before a stunned Egyptian court
was the product of thirty years of similar cutting.
Borrowing the southern woodcarver's concept, you could
say that God had taken a block of good wood and cut away
everything that wasn't charisma. This Joseph, in whom
was the Spirit of God, was no accident of the moment—no
coincidence of human events. The young man with the
impressive wisdom, foresight, and courage to speak truth
had been divinely groomed for this action right from the
very beginning. Every previous experience, every ounce of
pain, every humiliation in the past had sculpted a man
who was now shockproof. There had been no mistakes.

I visited with a man who is general manager in a plant
where strong, steel cable is manufactured. He took me out
among the giant machines designed to weave thin
strands of high quality steel together into a sort of rope that
can be utilized for the suspension of mighty bridges or the
lifting of modern elevators. The secret of the cable's
strength is in the high tension weave. Each strand is part
of the overall function of the cable's might. Woven together
they are a union of unbreakable resilience.

At peak performance, Joseph was like the woodcarving,
the end product of a cutting process that took years. God
had cut away all that wasn't authentic charisma. But Joseph
was also like a cable: strands of spiritual character
carefully woven together through experiences of increasing
stress. The carving, a thing of beauty; the cable, a thing
of strength. This was Joseph; this was God's work. The
search for Joseph's charisma must center on the pain of
cutting and the process of weaving.

The twin roles of slave and of prisoner seem now in
retrospect to have been ideal positions for carving and
weaving in a man's life. The positions held him in an

existential vise so that God could do his work. Held steady, with little room to move in any direction but that which God designed, Joseph had all his leadership abilities and insights polished and honed. At the same time an authentic charisma was being engendered. It was also being carefully restrained, held back in check until the moment when God, as master craftsman, wished for it to be fully revealed and released. There were no mistakes in the process which kept Joseph in the vise for ten or twelve years between Palestine and the palace even though he may have been tempted on a few occasions to think so.

Run the projector back again. Take another moment to speculate on the whys of Joseph's route to high leadership. Why did God choose a track which led through family rejection, slavery, and prison? We know Joseph's ultimate interpretation of that period: "God meant it for good," but still some of us may be urged on to muse upon the genius of the process, especially those of us who feel we are now in some sort of "jail," or living like a "slave."

Could it be that the process of cutting and weaving takes into account the familiar struggle many talented people have between the use of their natural gifts and gifts which are spiritual? It's obvious that from the very beginning Joseph has managerial talent. That might be developed quite quickly. But authentic charisma? The kind which confronts a nation? That takes longer to develop.

Suppose Joseph had never been locked in the vise where carving and weaving take place. Hypothetically speaking, suppose Joseph had gone straight from Palestine to the palace. Would there have been time and opportunity for the shaping of authentic charisma? Would there not have been an almost overwhelming temptation to "go it alone" on those natural abilities which seem so often to accelerate young men and women to premature success?

How often have we seen the multitalented young person rise quickly above the pack of his or her peers, ascending like a meteor only to suddenly fade into some sort of failure because a necessary moral or spiritual strength had never been developed?

Speculation again. If Joseph had been his own man during the years of his twenties, and if he had chosen to avoid the vise of slavery and prison, is it possible that he would have used his gifts in "good" pursuits but have perhaps missed the "best"? Again, is it possible that he would have slowly moved away from a direction that would have ultimately taken him to Pharaoh's palace and down lines of other successes? It is not that Joseph would have fallen necessarily into bad or evil ambitions. It is just worth asking if he would have been at the right place when a nation badly needed a man to show it how to avoid destroying itself.

If Joseph had skipped the vise, climbed quickly up the rungs of his natural abilities, would he have peaked too early, expended his creative energies, lost the edge that drives a person to perform at his or her very best?

Zoom in on that prison. It seems to have served several functions in Joseph's carving-weaving days. Obviously, it was a final proving ground, and it was of course a sort of funnel that paradoxically placed him geographically and relationally quite close to the palace. You have to see the prison as a kind of "waiting room" while events in the world slowly rose to a boil and demanded the qualities of leadership that Joseph had been groomed to offer.

But all of that is merely speculation, helpful perhaps in causing some of us to evaluate the "prisons" in which we sometimes find ourselves. Where would some of God's greatest servants have achieved their ministries if it hadn't been for the vise of a prison? Joseph is joined by some rather high-powered personalities when it comes to sharing prison in common. Jeremiah was hauled out of prison to confer with the king. Daniel enjoyed some of his best sleep in a prison surrounded by lions. John the Baptist lost his life but not his witness in a prison. Peter seems to have developed a habit of going and coming out of prisons more by his choice than that of the guards. And don't forget Paul who, much to the consternation of his captors, used prisons as places for song services, evangelism, church communications, and seminary training. Biblically speaking, prisons seem always to have been places for opportunities. Why do we who ache for Joseph-ministries in our homes, our congregations, our communities seek to avoid the "prisons?" Why do we wish to find God or have him find us in a "resort" rather than a "prison"?

To make a Joseph, God had to cut away that part of his family influence that ultimately might have caused him to become like his brothers or even what his father was like in earlier days. As we have already seen, God had to cut away certain freedoms for awhile so that he could hold Joseph tight to the bench. Perhaps you could say that he cut away premature success and potential relationships which might have dulled his appetite for the very best.

But what of that which God wove together? What are the strands that made the cable of Joseph's life so fully adequate to the occasions that were ahead?

Three outstanding characteristics of Joseph's development as a person were his sense of destiny, his integrity, and his commitment to excellence in the pursuit of all responsibilities. These three factors—actually the strands of the cable—are a progression or a spiritual growth process which, at full maturity, results in the authentic charisma displayed before Pharaoh and his nation.

Seen as a process of spiritual development, they suggest this sort of order. Joseph's childhood sense of destiny was the point of origin for his emerging inner integrity, and that in turn engendered a quality of excellence which permeated all of his work and relationships.

While one quality begets the other, at the same time it is important to observe that each of the three parallel spiritual factors continued to grow in and of itself. The three compare quite favorably to the steel strands woven together to form the virtually unbreakable cable. The thicker these strands, the stronger the cable. And with Joseph, the more mature the spiritual factors, the stronger the man.

But I think the theme needs one more step in its basic development. A further glance at these spiritual strands suggests that each points to a particular sector of relationship within the man himself.

The category of destiny, for example, speaks specifically to Joseph's keen awareness of God's place in his life. On the other hand, the category of integrity seems to speak to the kind of person Joseph saw himself to be. And out of these two comprehensions, one suddenly can observe that Joseph's commitment to excellence was a statement of his relationship to his world.

These three strands forming the cable of Joseph's charisma deserve a much fuller development. An understanding of their nature and implications might assist many of us in becoming aware of what might be required of us in future years. But again a warning might be important as we continue to turn the projector back and forth. Whether we seize the analogy of the cutting process or the analogy of the strands being woven together it would appear that this process happens only in the midst of pressure and pain. Remember the slaves' quarters; remember the jail. Remember the rejection; remember the temptation. For every crown there is a cross. And we cannot covet Joseph's charisma unless we accept his cross.

AXIOM FOUR
A person for turbulent times is convinced that his or her supreme
value is discovered in doing the revealed will of God. This alone
is genuine destiny: to make every encounter with the world an
opportunity to demonstrate, through word and deed, the
Creator's glory.

7/ A sense of destiny

Joseph always had a sense of being special. Admittedly, in
the beginning it would seem that he might have been wiser
to keep some of his thoughts to himself. But how much
can one expect out of a young boy? Knowledge and wisdom
do not always grow at the same speed.

One might even be tempted to think at first that Joseph's
ego was a bit overinflated, especially during those times
when he grated against his brothers' sensibilities with
reports of those dreams which always placed him front
and center while they filled only supporting positions.

But a study of the entire lifespan of Joseph puts
everything into a new perspective. God was, from the
beginning, impressing his own presence upon Joseph in a
mysterious process. The progressive awareness that the
young man had of God's place in his life is a thing of
beauty. It seems to have come in a deliberate series of easily
defined steps.

We know very little about Joseph's early theological

training. It is reasonable to assume that his father, Jacob, spent many hours conversing with his favorite son, passing on the oral traditions of the family. Joseph was probably well-schooled in the stories and their implications about his grandfather, Abraham, and the strange, even bizarre relationship between his father, Jacob, and his uncle, Esau.

Interwoven among these stories would have been the interpretations of their significance: God's calling of Abraham; God's miraculous promise of a son to a sterile father and a barren mother; God's odd guidance of events so as to extend the family birthright to Jacob and not Esau.

We assume that Joseph knew all of this and that it formed a backdrop to his own awareness of God's presence in his generation. Again it is between the lines, but one wonders if Jacob, in his presentation of the coat of long sleeves, did not take every opportunity to fill his favorite son's mind and heart with the thought that God would be calling him, Joseph, to carry on the family's special mission. Is this the "stuff" out of which the dreams of Joseph's destiny are created?

Joseph's biographer never bothered to give us the details of the young boy's doctrinal awareness of God. It seems enough to say that Joseph simply knew that events bigger than all of the family were going to conspire to put him into a special place of opportunity. There is no evidence that Joseph understood where, how, or when it would all happen, but he knew that one day he would actually speak for the family and provide the context of security in which it would live.

Perhaps in the brevity of the writer's words there is a message of subtle variety: that God begins his cutting actions not with loads of specific information and direction but rather carves in broad sweeps of the knife. The result is not a sharply defined doctrinal awareness of who God is and what he is doing, but rather a mysterious sense of his presence and that he will do his special work in times and methods that he alone chooses.

Perhaps all God wished for Joseph in those earliest days

was to experience that feeling of awe, that one's life is linked
to a living God who, at the right moment, will have more
to say.

The Lord is not specifically mentioned in Joseph's life
until he reached the home of Potiphar. There two facts of
significance emerge. One, that Joseph keenly felt the
presence of God leading him toward a successful climb in
the management pyramid of Potiphar's business. And,
second, Joseph's dramatic awareness of God's lordship over
him in the matter of Potiphar's wife's proposal.

The first of these two awarenesses is one of propulsion.
God's presence thrust Joseph forward, causing him
apparently to become bold in the implementation of his
gifts and abilities. Joseph's success is directly tied to the
presence of God in his life. Joseph and God seem to have
developed a living, personal relationship in which the
young man was quite sensitive to God's leading, to God's
laws, to God's approval. The result? Success in his work.

The second of these awarenesses is one of accountability.
"How can I do this thing and sin against God?" Joseph
cried out in the agony of what must have been a very
effective temptation. The writer made no mention that
Joseph was frightened over Potiphar's reaction should he
find out. He was not worried about whatever laws there
were in Egypt governing the matter of adultery. And Joseph
didn't seem to be concerned over whatever this sexual act
might gain for him or lose for him.

But what Joseph was greatly disturbed about is what
God might think. To sin against God would have been
unthinkable. And in acknowledging this fact, Joseph tells
us something. He was saying that his present and future
relied solely upon what God was saying to him and what
God asked of him. Nothing else by contrast really counted.
At this early age his destiny was entirely in the hands of
God.

When Joseph landed in jail, the result of an evil
woman's lies, the writer made another "Lord-was-with"
statement but now instead of commenting upon resulting
success, he wrote, "and showed him [Joseph] steadfast
love." The reader can almost feel the growing intimacy

between Joseph and God: success in the midst of
opportunity; comforting love in the midst of adversity.
Such a flow of ministry from heaven was bound once again
to further cement the ties between Joseph and his God.

The writer felt no need to tell us how the "steadfast love"
came to Joseph—only that it was there when Joseph
needed it. The two "Lord-was-with" statements within
this period of Joseph's life might lead one to think upon
the resulting experiences that come out of God's promised
presence in the life of his servants. Where God is, there is
effectiveness; there is steadfast love.

The appearance of Joseph in the court of the pharaoh
for the interpretation of the dream takes us another step
along in the cutting process in which Joseph became
increasingly resolute in terms of his relationship
to God. Joseph had learned something of considerable
importance when he said to Pharaoh, "It is not in me [to
interpret the dream]; God will give Pharaoh a favorable
answer."

Joseph's conviction of destiny has come to a point of
maturity in which he knew clearly the things God would do
in and through his life, using him simply as heaven's tool.
Joseph knew that his appointment with power and
responsibility had nothing to do with what he was but
rather what he was when God was residing within him.

That Joseph fully understood this is reiterated several
more times: "God has revealed . . ." "God has shown . . ."
And it reached a sort of crescendo at this point when
Joseph affirmed that "the thing is fixed by God, and God
will shortly bring it to pass."

Not only had Joseph asserted that God was speaking
through him as a person, but Joseph wanted the king to
know that the times, the processes of history, the events of
nature were in God's hand, and when God chose to
manipulate or interrupt it, whatever he willed would
happen. Joseph's theology is amazing. It is massive; it
is powerful; it is absorbing. And he plainly set himself in the
middle of it all and submitted himself to it.

Later when Joseph had set in motion his plan for the
economic salvation of Egypt, he became the father of two

sons. In the naming of the two boys Joseph once again gave indication of the carving work of God in his life, the constant refinement of this special charisma with which he's been endowed.

The first son was Manasseh, which means "God has made me forget all my hardship and all my father's house." I hear Joseph telling us that he had resolved all the past events of his life. His certain conviction that God had permitted all the past events and that they had been a heaven-designed track which permitted him to come to this point of service had freed him of any bitterness over the painful events of the past. Even resentment against his brothers who had conspired to make his life as miserable as possible was gone. "The Lord has made me forget."

The second son was Ephraim, a name of equal testimony to Joseph's relationship to God and its resulting destiny for him: "For God has made me fruitful in the land of my affliction." "*Fruitful*" is almost an understatement, seeing that he was at this moment the second most powerful man in Egypt. But what is most significant was Joseph's unqualified recognition, "God has made me." He affirmed at the summit of his success that everything he had, everything he had accomplished, everything that he had become was the result of God's shaping work in his life. God had simply carved away everything that wasn't charisma. This was the finished product. This is what God had created every person to be in principle, "Josephs" who live triumphantly through the cuts of the knife, accepting the process because of that destiny that lies beyond.

Two final statements of testimony by Joseph complete the case of his awareness of God's work in his life. The first appears when Joseph had a private interview with his brothers who had come to Egypt seeking food. He revealed himself to them saying,

And *God* sent me before you to preserve for you a remnant on earth, and to keep alive for you many survivors. So it was not you who sent me here, but God; and he has made me a father to Pharaoh, and lord of all his house and

ruler over all the land of Egypt. Make haste and go up to
my father and say to him, "Thus says your son Joseph, God
has made me lord of all Egypt; come down to me, do not
tarry; you shall dwell in the land of Goshen, and you shall
be near me. . . ." [Gen. 45:7-10]

"God sent me . . . God made me." Success had not gone
to Joseph's head. In a moment when most of us would have
been overwhelmingly tempted to flaunt the upper hand
over those who had conspired to make earlier life so
miserable, Joseph pressed into history a higher level of
meaning. What the brothers had done in selling Joseph into
slavery years before was in all actuality a sending action
by God. What the Egyptian system had done in oppressing
Joseph as a slave and a prisoner, God had used to make
him into something special.

With theological convictions like that, it is no wonder
that Joseph's sense of destiny never wavered. Nothing in the
history of his life was without meaning or purpose. And
in all of it he saw God doing special things for him and
through him.

Joseph's final statement about all of this comes much
later in life as he looked back on where his destiny had
brought him. It was made in response to a message sent to
him by his brothers who began to fear that when his
father died, Joseph would finally take the opportunity to
satisfy some residual pocket of vengeance that his
brothers suspected had always dwelt within his heart. That
they had this fear and projected it on Joseph is a
fascinating contrast to what they were as men and what
Joseph was. They simply couldn't come to grips with the
fact that Joseph would wipe from his mind and heart the
hostilities of former times. Even at this later date, they
seem to have felt that all of his words about God's work in
his life were simply a cover for what was really lurking
and waiting to get out at the right moment. Joseph's
reaction:

Fear not, for am I in the place of God? As for you, you
meant evil against me; but God meant it for good, to bring it

about that many people should be kept alive, as they are today. So do not fear; I will provide for you and your little ones. [Gen. 50:19-21]

And the writer concluded: "Thus he reassured them and comforted them" (Gen. 50:21).

In this final message Joseph once again indicated that he understood his relative position before God. He in fact was not God, and he knew it. He is convinced, as he always had been, that he was God's man in a turbulent situation, that he had responsibility toward God and toward those about him. This was his destiny, and he would not abuse it nor would he ever take it for granted.

AXIOM SIX
A person for turbulent times relentlessly pursues truth from every promising source. And having grasped any segment of it, he or she gladly resolves to press it immediately into daily performance. This person pays scant attention to those who watch either to applaud or condemn. When truth is the issue, the only goal is to please the One who is the Author of all truth.

8/ An unshakable and uncompromising integrity

As the tourist watches, the carver of the dogs takes from the shed what he has called "a good block of wood." To the untrained eye that watches, that "good block of wood" seems to be rough, ragged, and quite dirty. How can the carver see potential, he wonders, in something so unsightly?

The sharp knife in the hand of the mountain man begins its relentless motion across the surface of the wood First the bark is sliced away and then the outer surfaces fall chip by chip to the floor. And the knife, which at first had moved so swiftly and with seeming indiscretion, now begins to move much more slowly and deliberately. As the traveler watches, the grain of the wood appears; rough shapes become legs, a head, and a tail. The sculpted surface becomes smooth to the touch. A dog is appearing, just as the wood carver said it would. He knew his block of wood from the very beginning, and he never doubted what it could become. Now his shaping work is done.

One has a notion of that process as he watches thirty years pass in the life of Joseph. The heavenly Carver was doing his work, and the smooth surfaces of a man of God began to appear. Out of the inner intimacy in which a young man communed with his heavenly Father came the shape of an extraordinary person who possessed integrity. It is another of those steel strands which enhance the cablelike strength of the emerging person.

A newspaper classified ad seems to be hinting at integrity when it declares:

Northrup needs people who can see with fresh eyes; people who give no allegiance to accepted ideas; headstrong people; impatient for tomorrow.

What is it that Northrup seeks? Persons who it believes have built an independent base of inner spirit: who can make bold but sound decisions, lead task forces, and implement strategies without being swayed or pushed around by the random events and pressures of any given day or interest group. Northrup seeks integrity in addition to skill.

When *integrity* is used to describe the condition of an object, it means "put together properly and solidly." We say that a product has integrity if it will not disintegrate under normal pressure or stress. And we attribute integrity to that which provides reliable performance. These are some of the same things we seek to say of an individual upon whom we wish to depend.

All too often we have seen attempts to manufacture a sort of plastic integrity called image-making. Some politicians, for example, will be sure that much of their campaign advertising includes photos of them involved with their families, even though it is common knowledge that many politicians are among the country's worst family people. Some running for office manage to increase their rate of church attendance during the electioneering season. It is disturbing to realize that millions of dollars are spent within industry and government to sell the public on the so-called integrity of people in the spotlight. But all too often we discover to our discomfort that the integrity created by the image-makers is quite synthetic—certainly not spiritual.

It is in this very area—what a person is within themselves—that we have seen so much of the disintegration of Western society in the past two decades. The issue of integrity was front and center as we watched the fall of a president. The loss of integrity has given rise to public distrust of almost all of the important systems and structures of our national life. No one would refute the fact that there is a horrifying tidal wave of scepticism that greets anyone who speaks from a base of political or industrial power.

Perhaps the decline of integrity can be partially attributed to the fact that our social system has permitted, even encouraged, a divorce between the personal conduct of a public official and his required performance. It has apparently become an axiom within our society that the public has no right to examine an individual's personal life as a qualification for public office or employment. Successful performance has become the only valid criteria for evaluation.

It seems naive, however, to suppose that the ethics and morals of a person while at home will not sooner or later carry over to the job. Do we expect, for example, that a person who flagrantly practices infidelity toward his or her spouse will not under certain conditions also become unfaithful to some aspect of his or her business or political commitment?

Thirty years ago, Elton Trueblood was speaking to this issue when he wrote:

It is hard to think of any job in which the moral element is lacking. The skill of the dentist is wholly irrelevant, if he is unprincipled and irresponsible. There is little, in that case, to keep him from withdrawing teeth unnecessarily, because the patient is usually in a helpless situation. It is easy to see the harm that can be done by an unprincipled lawyer. Indeed, *such a man is far more dangerous if he is skilled than if he is not skilled.* We are accustomed to this

idea of moral responsibility in what we call the
professions, but something of the kind is a factor in more
common jobs. The house painter can cheat on his
materials, the well-paid workman can squander his time.
*Part of our present inflation in costs, which may
ultimately be so damaging to our society that collapse
follows, arises from such moral causes* (italics mine).
[*Your Other Vocation* (New York: Harper and Row, 1952)]

Trueblood is a prophet!

I do not think we can pass over lightly the fact that
much of the biographical material on Joseph centers on his
integrity and his obvious commitment to an ethical
creed. The writer was definitely choosing to tell us
something about the importance of the inner person that
one day would become the public person in the palace of the
pharaoh.

The roots of Joseph's integrity doubtlessly were
first his family background. As I mentioned earlier, we have
to assume that Joseph was quite well aware of events
during the past three generations covering the lifetimes of
his great-grandfather Abraham, his grandfather Isaac, and
his own father and uncle, Jacob and Esau. What he had not
learned from his father and mother, he probably heard
from his brothers on those occasions when there was a less
hostile atmosphere. Out of the family traditions must
have come many learning experiences which sank deep
into Joseph's spirit and became useful as he fended for
himself in the strange culture of Egypt.

Joseph probably knew the story of the choices made by
Abraham and Lot and how life in Sodom had slowly
drained Lot of all his accumulated resources. Did Lot's
susceptibility to Sodom's allure have any relevance to
Joseph as he worked through the propositions placed before
him by Potiphar's wife? Weren't there similarities, and
didn't Joseph have a chance to view the unfortunate
consequences of an ancestor's poor choice?

What might Joseph have learned from the agonizing
delay through which Abraham and Sarah lived as they
trusted God for a son who would continue the family

mission? Did their pain and heartache come as a source of renewal to him during the long years he spent as both slave and prisoner, rekindling his nerve to wait upon God for the divinely chosen moment when his own destiny would be realized?

Did the mysterious story of how Isaac was introduced to the beautiful Rebekah ever cross Joseph's mind as he was tempted to wonder if the God of heaven had lost interest in the details of his life in Egypt? And could Joseph have learned much from the tales of his own father's deceitfulness and its near destruction of the entire family? Did he consider the effects of all the family tragedies which had occurred as a result of his father's lies and his uncle's weakness? Were these some of the background factors that made Joseph develop a powerful respect for the truth? Did his own concept of loyalty in relationship grow out of his awareness of the effects upon the family each time there had been disloyalty?

Much of what Joseph's family had to teach him came from a negative perspective. He had learned more from their unfortunate consequences than from their right actions. But credit Joseph with making a break from the negative family traditions. God was able to pluck a sprout from an otherwise corrupt generation tree and make something beautiful of it. The heavenly Carver knows "a good block of wood."

We see evidences of Joseph's integrity first in his uncompromising attitude toward the truth. He wouldn't tamper with it. It's seen, for example, in the "ill report" that he brought to his father about his brothers' business dealings. I suspect that it was also present in his seeming compulsion to share with the family the contents of those irritating dreams of his childhood. The fact is that Joseph simply didn't believe in covering up anything.

This sort of honesty was obviously spotted by Potiphar when Joseph came to work as a slave. Joseph's commitment to truth was so complete that Potiphar did not hesitate to put everything to do with his business into the slave's hands. In a modern context we can picture Potiphar giving Joseph check-writing privileges, delegating authority

for buying and selling, hiring and firing. One can imagine
Joseph carrying an ancient version of a credit card wallet
that provided him with an unlimited expense account.

Again Joseph's respect for truth must have been observed
by the captain of the guard, the warden at the prison
where Joseph was sent. Is it wrongful speculation to
suggest that Joseph probably could have walked away
from the prison at any time that he chose? But he didn't
because he had integrity.

Integrity also speaks to the nature of Joseph's attitudes
toward those who treated him adversely: his brothers,
Potiphar's wife, ungrateful Potiphar himself, the king's
butler who forgot him in jail. There is simply never a
record of any kind of resentment, or of any sort of
premeditated vengeance. In fact Joseph seemed to have
been quite incapable of misdirected anger. He was the
perfect specimen of the self-controlled man.

As we have already observed, Joseph's encounter with
sexual temptation is a revealing commentary on his
moral integrity. His ability to maintain control over
powerful appetites and passions was exemplary. It serves
as a rebuke to a public spirit in our own age which not only
ignores those who freely indulge in that to which Joseph
said no, but tends to applaud and be amused by those who
do.

A further evidence of Joseph's integrity is seen in his
unswerving loyalty in all relationships. In his younger
days his loyalty was to his father, much to the
embarrassment of his brothers. Joseph would not keep
silent about the family business practices if his father was
going to be deceived and cheated or the family name
compromised. When his brothers created situations which
tested his loyalty, there was no question as to where he
would turn. His father was the immediate winner.

When faced with the temptation in Potiphar's house,
Joseph made it quite plain that he fully understood the
prevailing lines of loyalty. To the boss's wife he said:

Lo, having me my master has no concern about anything
in the house, and he has put everything that he has in my

hand; he is not greater in this house than I am; nor has he
kept back anything from me except yourself, because you
are his wife; how then can I do this great wickedness, and
sin against God? [Gen. 39:8, 9]

Although Joseph's ultimate loyalty was to God, he
certainly displayed within this statement his awareness
of a specific commitment to Potiphar which superseded
every other relationship.

No wonder the pharaoh gave Joseph the job of being
second in command in Egypt. His whole life had proved
that he understood lines of authority, objectives within a
job, and the importance of dependable performance. "Go
to Joseph," the pharaoh would later tell the people of the
realm, "what he says to you, do!" And all of this
accelerated in the final description of Joseph's job: "and all
the earth came to Egypt to Joseph. . . ." There is no record
that Pharaoh ever thought that Joseph might foment a
palace revolution or seize the kingdom.

If there is any final symbol of Joseph's integrity, it is in
those words of special affection and respect which he had
for his father. Sending his brothers back to their homeland
to retrieve their father, he said, "Go to my father . . . (tell
him) 'thus says your son . . . God has made me lord of all
Egypt . . . come down to me . . . you shall be near me.' "

There is a richness in that message of son to father that
suggests that although Joseph was in charge of virtually
everything in his world, he was still loyal to his own father.
He sought his father's love. He wanted his father to be
near, to see how he was carrying on the family dream, and
that he had become all that the father had ever dreamed
for him.

It is obvious that the heavenly Carver had done his job.
In Joseph one begins to see the grain showing in the wood
of authentic charisma. The shapes of such a man with
such charisma was becoming apparent. This was a charisma
that God had carved and it is beautiful to behold.

I find it somewhat intimidating to my spirit to place
these thoughts on paper for they not only remind me of
what I should be becoming as man, husband, father, pastor,

friend, but they rebuke me for what I am obviously not—at least yet.

Perhaps Joseph's professional success is out of reach for most of us—but his level of integrity is certainly not. There is nothing in his spiritual life which has not been faced in principle by all of us. God provides Joseph as a gift to us. We must be like him in integrity. It is the way to the authentic charisma much in demand but rare to observe in the turbulent eighties and nineties of our society.

AXIOM SEVEN
A person for turbulent times understands the significant
difference between excellence and perfection. He or she
emphasizes the former but eschews the latter. Choosing to be
found faithful, this person is least likely to be seduced by the
powerful sirens of success. With a formula for effectiveness
discovered on bended knees, he or she makes things
happen—excellently.

9/ Where the rubber meets the road

The tire company says that the final test of a good tire is
down "where the rubber meets the road." The tire may
have a good name, and it may have an attractive design, but
if it can't perform where the rubber meets the road, it is
worthless. Thousands of North Americans learned that
lesson the hard way when a tire with a great name and an
attractive appearance couldn't do the job on the road and had
to be recalled.

For the woodcarver who makes a living chipping away at
"a good chunk of wood," the final test is whether or not
the dogs are bought by the tourist. For the steel cable, the
final test is whether the braided strands are capable of
bearing the weight. And for Joseph, the final test in each
segment of his life—son, slave, prisoner, and prime
minister—was whether or not he could summon from
within the charisma that would meet the challenge of
each moment.

Authentic charisma is the ultimate effect of a person

whose sense of destiny and unshakable, uncompromising integrity lead to an excellence of performance. Even at this third point in the pursuit for authentic charisma, a decision must still be made. One must *choose* a performance level out of which the charisma that leads and changes will flow. One must choose.

John Gardner writes:

Some people have greatness thrust upon them. Very few have excellence thrust upon them. They achieve it. They do not achieve it unwittingly, by "doin' what comes naturally," and they don't stumble into it in the course of amusing themselves. *All excellence involves discipline and tenacity of purpose* (italics mine). [*Excellence* (New York: Harper and Row, 1961)]

One chooses excellence as a way of life because of motives and attitudes which flow from internal spiritual development: the sense of destiny or specialness and the integrity of personhood.

With Joseph, excellence became a way of life from the very beginning. There seems to have been no difference between his days at home with his family, his days at Potiphar's, and his days in the palace. Whatever faced him received the same basic standard of work.

It is time to take one final shot at Joseph's life, now asking the questions that center on performance. What did Joseph do that caused his authentic charisma to be felt wherever he went? The answer falls into three parts: the *role* he occupied, the *plan* he pursued, and the *needs* he set out to meet.

THE ROLE THAT LEADS TO EXCELLENCE

The reason for the utter consistency of Joseph's life lies in the role he assumed in each job. There never seems to have been a shakedown or readjustment period as he moved from position to position because he treated each responsibility in the same way. He approached his work in the role of a servant. There is no record that suggests that

Joseph thought more of himself or thought differently of himself when he was prime minister than when he was slave to Potiphar. That is very important!

The servant's role is the only one that consistently inspires excellence. Servants understand that they are accountable to someone else. They live not by their own standards but by those of someone else. Joseph was always aware that in the use of his gifts, he was serving someone. He served his father; he served Potiphar; he served the captain of the guard; he served Pharaoh; but, above all, he served God. That discovery is an important key to Joseph's charisma. Apart from it, he cannot be understood or appreciated.

It was Joseph's quality of spirit more than his skills that brought him to the top. What men saw in him was his driving desire to serve. Doubtless those who picked Joseph had seen many men before him with just as much talent. But they apparently had not seen those with the integrity and the willingness to look out for the boss's best interests.

The stories of star athletes who refused to place the interests of the team ahead of their own are not new to any of us. We've seen more than one exceptional passer or runner cut from a football team because he wasn't willing to support the others.

The role of a servant is that of creating and maintaining an environment in which those about him or her can become what God has created them to be. "Lo, having me my master has no concern about anything in his house," Joseph told Potiphar's wife. "He has put everything that he has in my hand." Joseph was rightfully proud of the fact that he had been able to free up his master, release him for other matters. With Joseph around, Potiphar had "no concern." That role both delighted Joseph and demanded of him an extraordinary level of performance lest he let Potiphar down and betray his master's confidence.

That servanthood role can transfer freely from Potiphar's house into our homes and minds—into our marriages and families; into our friendships and congregations; into the environment in which we do our work.

But it contrasts sharply with the role many think significant today. Jesus Christ described that contrast in these words to his disciples:

You know that the rulers of the Gentiles lord it over them, and their great men exercise authority over them. It shall not be so among you; but whoever would be great among you must be your servant, and whoever would be first among you must be your slave. [Matt. 20:25-27]

When Jesus said those words, was Joseph at all upon his mind?

I admit that I could have been intimidated into excluding this concept of the servant in my leadership profile of Joseph had I not come across the text of a speech given early in 1979 by Michael Maccoby of Harvard, also the author of *The Gamesmen*, a study of patterns of contemporary leadership and management.

In the speech, Maccoby expressed his concern for the leaders of the eighties and nineties. While his remarks were mainly centered in the context of the business world, his insights reach a broader context. While he acknowledged that he saw "hints" here and there of effective leadership that might fit the final two decades of our century, he did not seem optimistic that many suitable leaders were arriving on the scene. His search centered for those who could bring "inspiration" to the structures and systems of our society.

The ideal leader should bring out the best in people, supporting the ideal character of a particular culture and historical period. When an individual in a position of leadership has the wrong traits or presents an image discordant with the times, it follows that inspiration will be lacking.

Today the image of both the leader and the ideal character in America is in question. We are unclear about what is best in us and what it takes to bring it out.

What Michael Maccoby seeks as inspiration, I have
sought as charisma. He searches for those with the capacity
to "breathe" into modern people the desire to be their
very best. Such a person must have proper traits; he must
fit the times; he must be committed to bringing out the
best in human beings.

Maccoby doesn't seem sure that we have had that kind
of leadership during the past years. It's been, he writes, the
era of the "gamesman"—the leader who plays games
with ideas, objectives, resources, and with people. The
gamesman plays at leadership; he gets his "kicks" out of
making things work. In most cases he is never overly
concerned about what he is leading or even where he is
leading it. Just as long as he is successful; as long as he
can hang one more trophy over the fireplace of recognition;
as long as he is properly remunerated. In other words, the
gamesman is not unlike the football player who is involved
in nothing more than a game for which he gets paid.
Maccoby's gamesman works in a spiritual vacuum. For him,
to borrow a phrase, winning isn't everything; it's the only
thing.

But the leader of the turbulent future must be different,
Maccoby states. Our society has "had it" with the
gamesman who has performed in an ethical void. We have
seen enough of the vacuous results of the gamesman's
work which produces Watergates, recalls, and human
exploitation. A new kind of leader must emerge quickly.
And his or her concern must be for bringing out the best in
people—not winning for himself. For the new kind of
leader, winning will be that moment when the people he or
she serves fulfill their human potential.

Joseph could have told us all that 4,000 years ago. His
role as servant was standard operating procedure
wherever he went. No wonder he performed excellently.

The gamesman is not an alien within the Christian
community. One can see traces of the gamesmanship
entangling itself in vast areas of Christian activity. It is
an insidious influence that leads Christians to measure the
work of God in terms of numbers, square footage, and
popular acceptance. The Christian church will probably

not be a breeding ground for servants in the eighties and nineties because contemporary Christian theology does not seriously address the matter of servanthood as the prime role of the mature Christian.

We are not teaching our youth to be Joseph-servants; rather we have inadvertently taught them to pursue power, security, and the accumulation of the trappings of success. We have not taught ourselves to serve one another, and we've still not learned the meaning of the simple words of Paul to the Philippians, "Let each of you look not only to his own interests, but also to the interests of others" (Phil. 2:4).

With increasing effect the Christian church in the west has embraced the leadership of superstars, not servants. We have gathered ourselves to a theology which is really quite painless and emphasizes "me first." Today the theme that overrides any other is that of me first in blessings; me first in the feel-good experience of certain spiritual gifts; me first in terms of material comfort and rewards. The preoccupation of our gospel and of our prayers often turns toward insipid forms of deliverance dwelling upon sickness or financial failure and avoiding the very kinds of suffering and stress which made Joseph the man we admire him to have been. The bottom line of the contemporary gospel—the one that does not produce servants—seems to be "grab the crown; avoid the cross." Those who assume the role of a servant would never do this.

A glance backward at Joseph's role as a servant shows that never once did he ever manipulate himself toward a position. He seemed most content to fit into second place wherever he found himself. It was the hand of God—not his own—that elevated him at the end. He saw his only responsibility as that of serving with distinction. And that produced excellence of performance.

A MAN WITH A STRATEGY

Authentic charisma is not simply enthusiasm and the bolstering of sagging spirits. It is the result of excellence which is expressed in the ability to see the challenges and formulate a plan. Authentic charisma is marked by clear, measurable direction.

Nowhere is that more aptly illustrated than in what happened the day that Joseph walked into the chambers of the Egyptian pharaoh for the first time. He was surrounded by uneasy men who sensed that something dangerous was in the air. But they didn't know where to look or what to do. Thus, it was Joseph's turn.

First, Joseph heard out the dream and from it he extrapolated the correct issue. Simply put: there were seven years of prosperity ahead; and there were seven years of adversity ahead beyond that. A fourteen-year period fraught with serious turbulence. That was the issue. The question? What to do about it?

His second action: propose a solution. "Pharaoh, find a man and give him emergency authority to coordinate the efforts of the entire Egyptian economy. Don't limit his authority; don't question his judgement. Trust him!"

In minutes, Joseph had done what no one else was able to accomplish. A sharp mind filled with the Spirit of God had discerned both the issue and the proper response. In retrospect it seems to have been so simple. But no one else had figured it out, had they?

A search of the nation produced no one capable of fitting Joseph's strategy. No one wise enough; no one forceful enough; no one trustworthy enough. No one except the man whom God had been preparing all along: Joseph himself.

The late coach Vincent Lombardi often spoke of the importance of a leader who could step to the front and give direction when no one else could:

The strength of the group is in the strength of the leader. Many mornings when I am worried or depressed I have to give myself what is almost a pep talk because I am not going before that ball club without being able to exude assurance. *I must be the first believer,* because there is no way you can hoodwink the players.

Joseph was first *believer,* and when the pharaoh's eyes leveled upon him and offered him the job which would implement the strategy, he was ready to perform.

What Joseph did was according to a well-thought-out and well-managed plan. His was not the effort of a group of boys on a sand lot who gather in an informal football huddle and draw new plays with fingers in the sand. The elements of this strategy must have been taking their place in his head for years, although Joseph would have had no idea exactly where it would all be carried out.

As he assumed his new role in quarters quite different from the jail where he'd arisen that morning, there must have been a burst of insight as to what the preparatory years had all been for. He had done all this in the home of Potiphar although on a smaller scale. And he had been doing these kinds of jobs in the prison among rebellious and bitter prisoners. He who could manage slaves for a master and prisoners for a warden would know now how to manage a nation. The plan was the same.

Does the Christian have a plan? A plan for the managing of homes where marriages and families can be effective? A plan that speaks to a nation presently plan-less, the result of too many years of moral and spiritual drifting? A plan that speaks to the growth and development of thinkers, artists, communicators, and laborers? No plan; no excellence. No excellence; no charisma. No charisma; no ministry.

A MOMENT BY MOMENT AGENDA

Halford Luccock once wrote of a parade of soldiers in New York City who were coming home from World War I. The lines of marchers were so long, he noted, that the police occasionally had to stop the parade at various points during its passage in order to allow crosstown traffic to proceed from east to west.

During one such interruption, the police mistakenly allowed the drum major of a band to pass through the cross street but halted his band. The drum major didn't know that, because his magnificent strut and exaggerated motions kept him looking forward, oblivious of events behind. The leader and his band were soon separated by several blocks.

Luccock paints with words the ludicrous picture of the drum major marching on, thinking himself to be a stylish leader but having lost his following blocks behind.

In the final analysis, what is a leader anyhow? Is he the one that wears the uniform and goes through the official motions? Or did he cease being a leader the moment he inadvertently abandoned his followers to other circumstances? He may act like one, but he isn't a leader if he's not in touch with his followers.

A final key to Joseph's excellence which bred authentic charisma was his sensitivity to the exact needs of the people he led. He seems to have known how to say two things in the right way at the right time. The two things? Yes and no! Joseph's daily agenda could be boiled down to those two words. For seven years he had to tell people no so that for seven more years he could tell them yes.

If the contemporary and counterfeit version of charisma has been based on telling people what they want to hear, then perhaps the most startling ingredient of the "authentic charisma" about which I've tried to write is that it means sometimes telling people the very thing they don't want to hear—a no.

Joseph's task each day for seven years was to deny people the right to spend the top 20 percent of their unprecedented national prosperity. He had to ask them to conserve, to move from excessive and comfortable choices to disciplined life-styles. The modern equivalent of Joseph's effort is to convince a nation that its energy is in short supply, that everyone must slow driving speed to 55 mph, drop the thermostats to 65°, and turn a lot of lights off. Perhaps we can appreciate the problem Joseph faced. How do you convince any population to say no to self? And remember that he had to do this on the credibility of his own predictive authority: that there was a seven year decline period in the near future.

The matter of restraint—the saying of the no—is a spiritual matter. Every bit of managerial genius would have been worthless if Joseph had not been able to reach the spirits of the Egyptian people and cause them to resolve to cooperate. We have already seen in our own nation that laws alone do not get people to make the severe

disciplinary decisions that bring conservation. Legislation
reaches minds; but authentic charisma reaches spirits.

The daily agenda of the Christian and of the Church must
include a sensitivity to the people in each of our worlds
and a knowledge of when one must say no to self and no to
others. One of the prime reasons we can expect an
imminent collapse of Western society is found in the
inability of people to say no to themselves any longer. It is
hard to see how that collapse can be postponed if from
somewhere there are not people with the kind of
authentic charisma that says "march with me"; by my style
of life; by my own example, I will lead the way in showing
where and how we must say no to those things which
threaten our future.

Dr. A. W. Tozer wrote of a day in Christian history when
those sitting in judgment of Athanasius, a church father,
attempted to intimidate him by telling him that the
whole world was against him. But the old saint boldly
responded, "Then is Athanasius against the whole world."
Where are those who would speak to the issues of the age
with the resounding no when turbulent events, both great
and small, point toward the exploitation of people, the
delivering up of our souls to the consequences of evil, to the
bartering away of all that God has offered those whom he
created?

Seven years later Joseph also knew the right moment
on the agenda to say yes. And because he had earlier held the
disciplinary line when things were in abundance, the
barn doors now could be opened up in a time of famine and
people could be fed. All the world came to Joseph because
the famine was severe. It was the beginning of the
fulfillment of a boyhood dream. The sheaves and the
stars were indeed bowing down, not because Joseph had
wished it but because God had ordained it.

With typical restraint the biographer of Joseph speaks
little of the recognition which Joseph received during
those days in which he said yes. Perhaps nothing needs to
be said; it is obvious that people would have been filled
with gratitude for what Joseph made them do in the previous

years. His willingness to serve, his ingenious plan, his earlier no's, now made it possible for people to hear the yes.

Such was the man Joseph, a person for his turbulent times, and such was his authentic charisma. That same authentic charisma must today flow through a million homes, through a hundred thousand churches. It must be brought to bear upon relationships of all sorts. It must be felt in the world. But from what source will it come? Only God knows.

When God wants to drill a man,
And thrill a man, and skill a man,
When God wants to mold a man
To play for Him the noblest part,
When He yearns with all His heart
To build so great and bold a man
That all the world shall be amazed,
Then watch God's methods, watch His ways!
How He ruthlessly perfects
Whom He royally elects;
How He hammers him and hurts him,
Making shapes and forms which only
God Himself can understand,
Even while His man is crying,
Lifting a beseeching hand . . .
Yet God bends but never breaks
When man's good He undertakes;
When He uses whom He chooses,
And with every purpose fuses
Man to act, and act to man,
And it was when He began;
When God tries His splendor out,
Man will know what He's about!

[Dale Martin Stone]

The tourist returns from the back room to the front of the mountain gift shop. Once again he fondles one of the magnificent carvings. He feels its smoothness; notes its balanced proportions.

What has made it thus? "I take a block of good wood and carve everything away that obviously isn't a dog."

O God: I am content this day to be nothing more than a block of human wood. Give me grace to bear the pain of the necessary slicing of your heavenly knife. Give me patience to accept the duration of time it takes to complete the process. Give me wisdom to know the moment you prepare for me to act. Make me a person for turbulent times. And invest within me that authentic charisma which points humanity to you. Amen.

PART THREE
ISAIAH: A CONTEMPLATIVE SPIRIT FOR TURBULENT TIMES

AXIOM EIGHT
A person for turbulent times is in constant touch with people,
with events, with trends of thought and value, and with the
good and bad choices of the human race. Where there is chaos and
disintegration, he or she seeks to bring a corrective course. And
where there is goodness and justice, this person seeks to bring
affirmation and blessing.

10/ The incredible worlds of an ancient contemplative/ World one

Someone or some group had put the old prophet on the
spot. He had been saying some rather dangerous and
controversial things. Doubtless there were some who
probably questioned his patriotism and whether or not he
had the best interest of the nation in mind when he
relentlessly launched each prophetic broadside at the king
and those seated with him in authority.

So now it was Isaiah's moment to come up with some
sharp answers. The questions? Probably some like these:
What kind of an axe are you grinding anyway? What gives
you the right to stand there and tell an entire country that it's
wrong? Where did you get these troublesome ideas to begin
with anyway? And what makes you so sure that you've got
the last word when those with the expertise and in the
"know" think you're dead wrong?

Whether the questions were actually asked or simply
implied in the knowing smirks of an audience, Isaiah the

prophet must have felt compelled to give an account for the unique perspective he had on the world, national, and local affairs. It was true: again and again he had blasted away at every part of the establishment: its kings, its princes, its religious leaders, and its business people. Now he was prepared to share his reasons. Where had it all begun? "In the year that King Uzziah died. . . ." Circa 742-740 B.C. (Isa. 6).

This lonely work to which Isaiah had committed himself was no self-generated idea, nothing he had slipped into inadvertently. Definitely not! It had had a beginning point, and he could reach back to a date and say, "It began there." From that time forward he had seen things in a different light. His perspective upon people, history, God, and even himself had dramatically changed. In that year, when Uzziah died, Isaiah became a different man; he would never be the same again.

Isaiah is the model of a man in short supply, yet—like Joseph—in desperate demand for the turbulent eighties and nineties of the twentieth century. Most people wouldn't know that, and if you suggested the need for some Isaiah types, they wouldn't understand. And if they did, they would probably disagree anyway. Isaiahs are irritants within any society. As a result they are almost never praised, never admired, never copied. If they make *Who's Who*, it is only because, the editor suggests, they are newsmakers— even if they make the kind of news that makes the majority of the population uncomfortable.

Isaiah is the *contemplative* man. He hears what no one else hears; he sees what no one sees; he says what no one wants to listen to. His contemplative posture makes him a reflective sort of person. He has learned that there are some things best heard in silence. He can survive for long periods of time without the company of fellow human beings while he communes with the whispering God.

The contemplative man deals in ideas and realities so awesome, so beyond the thought of the average person, that he must express himself in mysteries, in visions, in symbols. Ordinary words are far too limited. So attuned is he to what lies under the everyday façade that mankind constructs for itself, that he often builds up a head of enormous spiritual pressure. Thus, when he speaks, his voice may be saturated with anger; his illustrative actions strange, even embarrassing. It is as if he lives in two worlds: the one that belongs to man and the one that belongs to God.

The contemplative man has sensitive spiritual fingertips like the proverbial safecracker who can feel the slightest movement of the tumblers behind the dial on the vault. That sensitivity is jarred when God speaks in his ear, and it reacts, sometimes with pain, when it senses the hidden motives, the false assumptions, and the hypocritical justice practiced within the human family.

Isaiah is the contemplative. We don't need many like him in any generation. But we certainly need a few.

While official prophets will always be few in number, we need not be limited from the development of many with a prophetic posture in the world. And such a person will be first a contemplative. Isaiah marched to the drumbeat of heaven and was at the same time able to discern why the world's parade was not only out of step but also headed in the wrong direction. Such wisdom is not taught or bought. It is a grace of heaven received by an open heart.

Modern Christianity knows little about contemplative faith. It is much too absorbed in theological systems, right doctrines, and acquired knowledge. The contemplative Christian does not fit within the frantic, pressure-filled life of twentieth-century Christianity. And that is frightening, for we need the contemplative badly to tell us what he has seen and heard, that which has escaped the average eye and ear.

Isaiah, the contemplative prophet, deserves to be studied and appreciated. A refined model of what we need today, he can speak from the past to the men and women of the future and tell us what we need to hear.

THE DRAMA

When *did* it all begin? What had happened to spring Isaiah into his unanticipated role? The beginning of his description

is not overloaded with words. Simply the mating of two
events: one, known to the entire populace, the other, very
personal and private. But even in the union of the two
matters in one sentence, Isaiah is warning that what is
happening in one world is not always as significant as what
is happening in another. "In the year that King Uzziah died
[world one], I saw the Lord . . . [world two]."

Anyone in the crowd hearing those words knew
immediately about the year of which Isaiah spoke. It was
one of those years that stand out in anyone's lifetime. The
year's events were so far-reaching that no one would ever be
the same again. Talk about turbulence! It must have been
similar to the year President Kennedy died.

"Do you remember what you were doing when you got
the news?" someone asks when the subject of the
President's death comes up. We all nod our heads, if we were
around then. We remember because the news was so
stunning. And nothing has ever seemed quite the same
since.

Perhaps it was that way for those who, like Isaiah, lived
during the year Uzziah died. Why? Because King Uzziah
had been around for a long time—fifty-two years to be exact.
But what made his death even more spectacular and
memorable was the way that it happened. Thirty years after
he had been buried, people would acknowledge that life
was never the same again.

SCENE I: THE AMAZING UZZIAH

Uzziah had been a success from the beginning. When he
assumed the throne, he had nowhere to go but up. His
father, Amaziah, had been a disaster as a king. Under the
father's twenty-nine-year leadership, everything but the
national debt had gone down: the power of the nation; the
morale of the people; the spiritual temperature. Amaziah's
tendency to other gods had finally disgusted even his closest
followers so much that they jointly determined to
dethrone him. Seeing what was about to happen, Amaziah
withdrew from the palace, perhaps in a way similar to
another recent, well-publicized withdrawal from our

American capital. Amaziah fled southward to a garrison
town called Lachish. He should have kept going because
when he was discovered there, he was murdered and his
body was returned to Jerusalem for state burial.

After that violence, Uzziah, Amaziah's son, became the
new king. At sixteen years of age! It is hard to believe the
young teenager would remain on the throne for the next
fifty-two years and that he would elevate the nation of Judah
to unprecedented heights, matched only by the kingdoms
of David and Solomon.

As a king, Uzziah breathed new life into a demoralized
nation. He seemed to characterize the kind of vision that
could ignite the spirits of people. They followed him, and
they believed in him. As an administrator, he apparently had a
capacity to grasp the big picture of what a nation could be
like economically. Trade routes were reestablished;
agriculture was stimulated. He loved the soil. Tribes
enjoying Judah's protection along the borders paid tribute to
Jerusalem's treasury.

As a military commander Uzziah was peerless. The army
he put together was well-organized, well-equipped, and
well-trained. Uzziah's research and development people
provided modern weapons while his engineers designed
and constructed new fortifications and defense perimeters.
Nothing was left to guesswork.

The secret behind Uzziah? "He set himself to seek God in
the days of Zechariah, who instructed him in the fear of
God; and as long as he sought the Lord, God made him
prosper" (2 Chron. 26:5). The world around soon became
aware of the young Uzziah. "And his fame spread far, for he
was marvelously helped, till he was strong."

The tiny word "till" ought to be underlined, however,
because it apparently symbolizes a peak point in Uzziah's
life.

Whether it was an instant in time or simply a slow,
almost undiscernible process, we don't know, but
something happened to Uzziah when he became aware of
this acquired strength. As so often arises in the human
condition, this strength of his seemed to crowd out his
discipline of pursuing God and tempted him into becoming

more impressed with himself and his own resources. Conceit, pride, and self-satisfaction became the order of Uzziah's life.

It was probable that almost no one in Jerusalem except, of course, Uzziah's most intimate associates, was aware of the shifting of the king's spiritual foundations. As is so often the case, the image of the spiritual man would probably have been maintained until something unexpected and embarrassing happened one day that ripped away the mask and shocked the masses.

"But when he [Uzziah] was strong, he grew proud to his destruction. . . ." The mask came off the day the king strode proudly into the temple, with a bright idea. He would burn incense before the altar of the Lord, something law and precedent said was never done by anyone but the priests. There were eighty of them available at the time, so Uzziah could hardly have argued as King Saul had once done, saying to Samuel, "You weren't around, and I couldn't wait; so I went ahead and did it myself."

The Scripture is not specific about the meaning of the events surrounding this moment of confrontation between the king and the priests. It assumes that we understand the implications of Uzziah daring to cross carefully defined boundaries that had always before created a balance of spiritual and political power between the temple and the palace. If Uzziah got away with his action, the power balance would be seriously damaged, as well as God's law violated.

Why did Uzziah do it? Were the priests privy to Uzziah's actual spiritual condition so that they had refused to engage in spiritual exercise for his benefit? Was Uzziah bored, looking for new territories of power to conquer within the realm? Or was his level of conceit, now so incredibly high that he felt no necessity to subordinate himself to anyone else, even priests?

The confrontation between Uzziah and the eighty priests led by their chief, Azariah, was ugly. They apparently stood between the king and the altar, creating a human wall that would bar the way. But they only managed to kindle a kind of anger which erupts from hurt pride, because Uzziah became all the more determined that no one was going to tell him what to do. Taking the ceremonial censor he had carried into the altar room, he must have started forward in his fury, perhaps even with the intention of hitting the first priest who got in his way. But he never came a step farther toward the altar.

Scripture says that at that instant the white blotches of leprosy spread out upon his forehead. He must have felt it; the priests saw it. The unmasking was complete! One can imagine the dramatic tension that gripped every person in the room. The shock, the horror, people frozen to the spot where they stood as the awful truth of what was happening became plain.

Uzziah was "thrust out" of the temple, Scripture says. There is no recorded resistance by the king or his aides. By the end of the day he was not only gone from the temple but from the palace, not only stripped of spiritual privileges but no longer king, for all practical purposes. "And being a leper [he] dwelt in a separate house; for he was excluded from the house of the Lord. And Jotham his son was over the king's household, governing the people of the land."

Soon after, Uzziah was dead. Fifty-two years is a long time, and the majority of people in Judah had never known another king. The years had come and gone in a country where there had been unity, security, and continuity. For many, Uzziah must have seemed like a fixed star by which to navigate national and personal life. With him in charge there had never been a need to be concerned about tomorrow. But now he was dead, and he was buried in disgrace, buried not as a king but as a leper. You could say an ideal had also gone to the grave with him.

Perhaps now we can appreciate the state of national shock the year that King Uzziah died. Now we can begin to use some imagination and reconstruct what was going on in the mind of Isaiah, the coming contemplative, when he tells us that his life changed in the year that the great king died.

The year that King Uzziah died, Isaiah told those who were interested, "I saw the Lord. . . ." Already Isaiah speaks in riddles. Who "sees" an invisible God? But

contemplatives employ sensual words in spiritual ways.
They have eyes which are not eyes, and they see what
cannot be seen. When Isaiah said he saw the Lord, believe
him. He did!

The fact that Isaiah saw the Lord in the year that King
Uzziah died ought not to be passed over too quickly. At
least two things ought to be pondered about the mating of
the event and the vision.

First, Isaiah may be subtly telling us that, like everyone
else, he had never seen the Lord before Uzziah's death.
He may have trusted the strong Uzziah so much that he had
not given serious thought as to whether there was a
difference between Uzziah's ways and God's.

In the wake of a strong leader there is often a sort of
secondary idolatry: people guilty of believing more in the
leader than the leader's God. Is Isaiah hinting at this
possibility in his own life?

Could he be telegraphing to us the fact that it was only
when Uzziah was removed from the scene and when there
seemed to be no one who could match him, that Isaiah
had nowhere else to look but to God? Isn't that a familiar
spiritual phenomena? That people only struggle to see
the Lord when the carpet, so to speak, has been pulled out
from under them?

In dating his start as a prophet in the year King Uzziah
died was Isaiah telling us something about the deliberate
design of the God of Israel, who foreknew that Judah was
about to face a tremendous upheaval in its national life?
Would it need a new kind of prophet to help it face the real
issues of its day?

Perhaps Isaiah doesn't even realize what he was telling us.
But amidst the luxury of retrospect, we can now see once
again how God places a man upon the stage of every period
of history to be his spokesperson. Isaiah was to be the
man who would speak to men about God and to God about
men for the next fifty years.

Those fifty years which spanned the prophetic ministry
of Isaiah were turbulent with change. A succession of
four kings—Uzziah, Jotham, Ahaz, and Hezekiah—made
their marks upon the affairs of Judah, often to the

spiritual detriment of the people. Outside the borders of
the kingdom major empires expanded and periodically
clashed, sometimes using Judah as their rendezvous for
battle. It was a time for threats, confrontations,
accusations, betrayals, inflated egos, outright terror. There
was nothing dull about the days of Isaiah's life. It was a
period of history not unlike the time in which we are living.
How a man comported himself in such a historical and
spiritual context 2,700 years ago may shed light on the
necessary inner structures of life that Christians need to
develop today.

SCENE II: THE GATHERING STORM

Picture a wheel imposed upon the geographical landmass
of the Middle East, and place the hub over the city of
Jerusalem. To the immediate north of Judah (sometimes
called the Southern Kingdom) was Israel, often called the
Northern Kingdom. Its capital was the city of Samaria. The
two kingdoms had been divided since the days of
Solomon's sons and there had been little love lost between
the two states.

To the northeast of Jerusalem, at one or two o'clock on
the wheel, was Syria, with its capital in Damascus, and
well beyond the Syrians in the northeast direction was the
formidable empire of Assyria, perhaps the most powerful
political entity of Isaiah's lifetime. From its capital at
Nineveh, enormous armies known for their unbridled
cruelty had marched. The Assyrians were the bullies of the
era.

The young upstart empire of Babylon lay directly east of
Jerusalem, perhaps at about three o'clock on the wheel.
Its day was yet to come, and Isaiah was perceptive enough to
see long before anyone else that it was Babylon, not Assyria,
that would make Jerusalem sweat and suffer.

To complete the geopolitical encirclement of
Jerusalem is to look southward to Egypt, where a dynasty
imposed by the Ethiopians sat upon the ancient throne.
The pharaohs desired Judah, to their north, which was just
strong enough to form a protective buffer against

aggression from Assyria or Babylon. Thus it was in their best interest to offer the kings of Jerusalem alliances that would provide material and troops should Judah ever be threatened. History would show that Egypt looked better on paper than it did on the battlefield, much to the consternation of those in Jerusalem who believed just the opposite.

The western side of Jerusalem's "wheel" was the sea, and it completed the limits of Judah's world. It became a sort of anvil upon which the surrounding nations would attempt to beat Judah to pieces.

This geography lesson is important because around the time of Uzziah's death events set in motion by these nations began to envelop Judah in foreign politics to an extent that it had never known before. For centuries Jerusalem had maintained a traditional aloofness from its big power neighbors to the north, east, and south. And conversely, they had never seriously bothered Jerusalem. What international activity there had been was mainly centered on the troublesome tribes living along Judah's borders that had never been fully subjugated. The result was, in Isaiah's day, that the nation's people and its leaders had accumulated little experience in dealing with other foreign powers.

The political skies began to darken somewhere around 735 B.C., four or five years after the death of Uzziah. Jotham, Uzziah's son, had lasted only a few years and was then dead. He had been succeeded by Ahaz, a young man spiritually rebellious against God from the very beginning. Ahaz had no sooner gained control of the kingdom when he was confronted by an invitation from the kings of Israel and Syria to join a growing coalition of smaller nations that wished to attack Assyria. For years Assyria had exacted heavy tribute from their treasuries, and now the Syrians and the Samarians saw the possibility of divesting themselves of Assyrian hegemony. The key to their success would be cooperation from Ahaz.

After he weighed the relative merits of the offer, Ahaz said no. After all, he was not being pressured by the Assyrians, so it made little sense to get involved. When his refusal was received by his northern neighbors, Ahaz felt the beginning of political heat that would affect him for the rest of his life.

When Ahaz balked at the invitation to join the anti-Assyrians, the kings of Israel and Syria, Pekah and Rezin, decided to take action against him. Assuming that military force would topple the government in Jerusalem and put a man into power that would see things their way, these two kings marched their troops into Judah and systematically occupied most of the kingdom until they reached the gates of Jerusalem.

There was sheer panic in the city. Ahaz seemed destined to defeat, the city ripe for the plucking of the Samarians and the Syrians. The hearts of the people and their king "shook as the trees of the forest shake before the wind" (Isa. 7:2). Determined to hold out to the last, Ahaz sent envoys to Tiglath-pileser III, king of the dreaded Assyrians, asking for help.

He got what he asked for, but at a great price as we'll see later. Soon armies from Nineveh managed to neutralize every member of the once heady anti-Assyrian treaty organization. For Ahaz in Jerusalem there was great relief. They could breathe again. Ahaz had made an enormous political gamble; he had played for high stakes on the international scene, and he had won, so it seemed.

Of course there was a price. Nothing is free, and Jerusalem began to learn that when Ahaz journeyed north to the defeated Damascus to meet and express appreciation to Tiglath-pileser III of Assyria. Second Kings 16 indicates that Ahaz returned from that meeting overawed by what he had seen and heard. He couldn't wait to duplicate the splendor of his Assyrian idol, the king who had rescued him. He made radical changes in the Jerusalem temple and its form of worship. He reconstructed altars, patterning them after ones he had seen among the Assyrians. There seemed to be no restraint in adapting to the ways of the Assyrians who had become his friend. Although Ahaz didn't realize it, it was the down payment of an increasing higher price for playing big power politics.

Kings die, like all common men, and the great

Tiglath-pileser III died in 727 B.C. The irrepressible people of the Northern Kingdom of Israel leaped to the occasion, thinking to take advantage of the power vacuum they expected in Nineveh. They ceased making the heavy tribute payments to the Assyrians.

To the south in Jerusalem, Ahaz was dead. His replacement was Hezekiah, a king with every intention of purifying the temple that Ahaz had polluted and restoring the nation to spiritual fidelity. But perhaps Hezekiah was not strong enough, and perhaps the people themselves had become too exposed to other ways. The renewal that Hezekiah launched lasted only a short while and in the end even Hezekiah grew spiritually cold.

SCENE III: ON THE TRAIL TO DISASTER

The Northern Kingdom, Israel, had made a bad decision when it twitched the Assyrian nose because Sargon II, Tiglath-pileser's successor, came south with vengeance in mind. When he finished in 722 B.C. Israel no longer existed. Its people were uprooted and transported back to Assyria, their national life was ended. They should have kept paying the tribute.

Now the international winds began to blow with tornado-like force in the years that followed. The Babylonians, growing resistant toward Assyria, sent envoys to Jerusalem to pay a courtesy call on Hezekiah. The real reason, however, was to sound him out about a new alignment that might tip the power balance against the Assyrians. It was apparently an offer that Hezekiah couldn't refuse, because he didn't. The agreement was settled.

At the same time Hezekiah sent messengers to Egypt to open up negotiations that might eventuate in their assistance. Knowing that this might bring war to his doorstep, he turned Jerusalem itself into an armed camp, fortifying and preparing it for all the possibilities of protracted warfare. Between the treaties and the military preparations, things couldn't have been brighter for Hezekiah. It appeared that he had put everything together. Nothing could go wrong.

The world war got underway in 703 B.C. Assyria, now under another king, Sennacherib, first moved against the Babylonians and won. Then it headed westward systematically eliminating its opposition, nation by nation. When it turned south it whipped the Egyptians, forcing them back behind their borders.

Then it was Jerusalem's turn. Judah was a pushover from the day the Assyrian army arrived at the borders. Soon the army of the king of Assyria was at Lachish, sending messengers to Jerusalem, suggesting that a surrender was appropriate. Hezekiah responded with an offer of willingness to pay heavy tribute but Sennacherib wanted more; he wanted Jerusalem.

The biblical description of confrontation between Hezekiah's people and Sennacherib's people at the walls of Jerusalem as they discussed surrender terms is fascinating. The Assyrians fully understood the complete vulnerability of Hezekiah. There was nothing to prohibit the Assyrians from marching in and taking what they wanted, nothing except miraculous intervention.

And that is exactly what happened! A devastating disease swept the Assyrian army camp and forced Sennacherib to withdraw before he could effect Hezekiah's surrender. He went home to Nineveh where he was subsequently murdered by his sons. But for almost seventy-five more years, Judah became a nation living under the mercy of the Assyrians who required of it every available ounce of tribute possible. But ironically it would finally fall to Babylon.

The seventy-five years were turbulent years. Judah was a has-been. It would never again see the days of a David, a Solomon, or a Uzziah. *World One* was in shambles.

Isaiah lived through almost all of those events and what he saw, what he did and what he said provide amazing insights into the kind of person for turbulent times a comtemplative prophet can be. His day was not unlike ours. His problems similar to ours. What was his mission? An important question!

AXIOM NINE
A person for turbulent times is regularly seeking to be in touch with the living God. This is a person who, like Moses, has struggled to the mountaintop and returns, mirroring the heavenly Presence, to report and reflect the glory of the Creator.

11/ A different perspective altogether/ A second world

A commingled sense of mourning and shock must have paralyzed the city of Jerusalem the year that King Uzziah died. A bewildered populace must have pondered long and hard over the double impact of the irreplaceable loss of a great leader and the disillusioning reports of the events surrounding his death. The year would be the great measuring point in the passage of time for that generation.

But for Isaiah, the events of that year would have a different impact. For him, it was the year that "he saw the Lord." While for everyone else it was the year of demise, for Isaiah it was the year of vision as he caught a glimpse of the presence of the Holy One of Israel, the Everlasting God.

Isaiah's account was a description of a momentary renewal experience. He was describing a confrontation that would have a lifetime of impact. Out of it would come a reprogramming and a reprioritizing of all his spiritual sensitivities.

The major result? Having seen the Lord, Isaiah would begin to see his world from an entirely different perspective. Events and personalities would be weighed on a different scale. When the majority would come to one conclusion, Isaiah would come to another. What others would call success, Isaiah would label as failure. And what still others would consider disaster, Isaiah would curiously see as success and victory. It is strange what happens when a man has the sort of confrontation with God that Isaiah experienced.

Isaiah's vision is worth studying. If it is true that there is a desperate need for contemplative Christians, then it follows that we must appreciate what it was that launched Isaiah on the path he pursued. Thankfully, he has described his experience in as vivid detail as language will permit.

If you ask the scholars to vote on the actual site of this vision they would be equally divided. Did it happen in the actual temple of Jerusalem? Or was this a temple fabricated within the prophet himself as Isaiah met God in the privacy of a comtemplative experience? Did it happen at night or day? Was it real in terms of space and time, or was it imagery of unlimited scope, indelibly written upon the prophet's inner spirit? Don't vote; don't worry about it. Leave the surface analysis to the experts. Rather, turn your attention to the fact that the vision happened to a person and that its effects upon him were real and enduring.

The first sight in the vision was that of the Lord, "sitting upon a throne, high and lifted up, and his train filled the temple." Every word in this opening statement radiates with power and majesty, the symbols of a king. Remember that this scene of heavenly royalty is set in the backdrop of the grim reality of Uzziah's death. At this same time, Jerusalem's people are walking city streets asking each other, "What do we do now? Can anyone really fill the shoes of the great Uzziah?"

But in the vision of Isaiah, a statement is being made by the scene's imagery that mocks Jerusalem's panic. Uzziah may be dead, but Jerusalem has never really lost its greater King. Death may have conquered the royal power in the palace but it will never be on the agenda in the "temple" where God the Eternal King dwells.

The royal symbols? Kings sit, while the entourage stands. Others have only chairs; the king has a throne. And while seated upon that throne he issues edicts and judgments which are unquestioned by all who are in the embrace of his power.

The writers of the Old and New Testament frequently seized upon two symbols of power: the throne and the altar. A king sits upon the throne; a lamb is spread across an altar. One symbol complements the other. The one who sits upon the throne entering Isaiah's world will one day enter the rest of the world as a lamb. Isaiah himself would foresee that event later on in his writings.

The heavenly King that Isaiah saw in this vision was not only separated from others by his posture of sitting upon a throne of authority and power, but he was separated from others by height. He was above and he was on a level above which no one will reach.

There are exceptions of course. Later on in his prophetic utterings, Isaiah would recall the attempts of heaven's archenemy "Day Star, son of Dawn." His acts are characterized in these words:

You said in your heart, "I will ascend to heaven; above the stars of God I will set my throne on high; I will sit on the mount of assembly in the far north; I will ascend above the heights of the clouds, I will make myself like the Most High." [Isaiah 14:13, 14]

Don't overlook Isaiah's view of God as "high and lifted up." It would forever sensitize him toward any futile effort, by Satan or any other creatures, to so elevate themselves that they might presume to share or even usurp God's throne.

With an inner image of his God so high above all things, one can now begin to understand why Isaiah looked upon the international flutterings of Jerusalem's kings, Assyria's military commanders, and Babylon's diplomats, and why he prophetically smiled at their efforts to impress their generation.

By contrast it becomes clearer as to why Ahaz and
Hezekiah of Jerusalem became so easily intimidated by the
Tiglath-pilesers and the Sargons of Assyria. Their
calibration of "high and lifted up" began at Nineveh. They
had seen nothing higher. But Nineveh's power was
infinitesimal compared to the heavenly King Isaiah
confronted in the temple. Thus, when forced to make a
choice between the power seen in this visionary temple
and that projected in the palaces of the international
scene, Isaiah didn't have the slightest bit of difficulty
determining which impressed him the most.

Leonard Griffith spotlights this one-sided power
confrontation between the world of Jerusalem and the
world of the visionary temple and writes as a Christian:

I saw the Conquerers riding by
  With cruel lips and faces wan:
Musing on kingdoms sacked and burned
  There rode the Mongol Genghis Khan;

And Alexander, like a god,
  Who sought to weld the world in one;
And Caesar with his laurel wreath;
  And like a thing from Hell, the Hun;

And leading, like a star the van,
  Heedless of upstretched arm and groan
Inscrutable Napoleon went
  Dreaming of empire, and alone. . . .

Then all they perished from the earth
  As fleeting shadows from a glass.
And, conquering down the centuries,
  Came Christ, the Swordless, on an Ass!

This then is the view of God which reached the eyes of
Isaiah's contemplative heart. From henceforth, the power of
the establishments in his world would be relative,
measured only against the power of the King in the temple
who sat in lofty places of unparalleled height.

When Isaiah saw this vision he began with a wide-angle
lens perspective. His eyes had been riveted first on the

King. Now he scanned the entourage that crowded this
special place. This was the heavenly family, filling the
temple. And among the magnificent train were the
seraphim, Isaiah said. It is hard to be exact about their
identity. Are they angels or celestial mortals of some kind?
It is difficult to discern. In this vision their role is that of
glorifying the King; they are the leaders of a never-ending
worship which takes place in God's presence.

The vision of Isaiah now struggles for words. There are
some things the contemplative cannot put into simple
terms. But Isaiah strained to do justice to what he saw and
heard. Perhaps only the contemporary contemplative
can adequately decode the account to the ancient
contemplative and extrapolate from the description the
fullness of its meaning. Those of us who demand a technical
and material description are headed for disappointment.
Some of us are needlessly restless in the presence of
mystery and we shouldn't be. Contemplatives know that
mysteries have a humbling effect. Does this explain the
discomfort of some who fear a mystery?

Surrounding the heavenly King for the purposes of
praise, the seraphim employ their wings in a way that
can only be faintly understood. That they are "above" the
King is not the same presumption that we thought of a
moment ago. Rather they are above him in that they are
framing the Lord with reflected glory.

"Each had six wings," Isaiah wrote. With one pair each of
these heavenly beings covered his feet; with a second pair
they covered their faces; and with the third pair they flew.

The nineteenth century English preacher Charles
Simeon contemplated this vision and wryly suggested that if
an Englishman had created it, he would have pictured the
seraphim as flapping all their wings furiously in a frantic
pace so as to actively *serve* the King on the throne.
Simeon is insightful when he recalls that the normal human
tendency is to interpret worship and praise as an act of
motion and busyness. But such, Simeon added, was not the
way the heavenly family saw worship.

Four of the six wings of each of the seraphim were used for
acts of covering; only two were used to move above.

Simeon suggests that the draping of the feet with two wings symbolically reflected an unworthiness to even serve this King. That we are privileged to serve God is an act of grace. Perhaps, Simeon further reflected, the covering of the eyes speaks to the unworthiness of even the seraphim to behold the majesty of God—something most of us presume we may rightfully do. Thus, even the opportunity to worship the living God, to drink in the fullness of what glory he chooses to reveal to humanity may itself be an act of heavenly grace, something most Christians rarely ponder. The seraphim, by covering their feet and eyes, are telling us that humbleness is a requirement for the contemplative—for anyone who seeks to draw near to the throne.

Only the third pair of wings is used to fly, speaking perhaps of the activities of service. If we can assume that this is the correct message of the symbolism of the wings, one can just about begin to grasp how out of balance is the brand of modern activistic Christianity many of us embrace—one which exalts busyness in motion, putting a relatively low premium on the disciplines of the contemplative.

The liturgy in the temple is not that only of position and symbolism. The seraphim are not silent; they begin to speak. "They called to one another," Isaiah wrote. Their actions and their words reflected that which they knew the heavenly King to be.

In that they called to one another, the seraphim have something to teach contemplatives of all generations, beginning with Isaiah. They tell us that worship is in part the act of the people of God speaking to one another "in psalms, hymns, and spiritual songs. . . ." about who God is, what he has done, and what he requires. It is a marvelously restorative experience, this "calling out to one another."

In such worship we speak to one another about God and in doing so we recalibrate our spiritual perspectives.

Isaiah gives us the essential subject of the "calling" of the seraphim. "Holy, holy, holy is the Lord God of Hosts; The whole earth is filled with his glory." If Isaiah had to boil down the theology of the heavenly family to two sentences, he chose well the words he transmits to us.

The first phrase underscores the holiness of God. Only when contemplatives withdraw from the interfering static of modern commerce can they even begin to comprehend the message of this term. To speak of God's holiness is to employ concepts such as perfect, complete, stainless. But even these words are far too inadequate to convey to us the fullness of the meaning of the word *holy*.

The contemplative exhausts all words and symbols in the exploration of the depth and breadth of God's holiness. It finally becomes enough to say that *holy* speaks to the entirety of God's nature of being. By saying that God is holy the worshiper affirms that God is everything the worshiper is not. This is an awesome insight and cannot be treated with anything but ultimate seriousness. For should we ever presume—in our human state—to approach a holy God, it would be as if we who are unholy ventured too close to the sun. Our imperfections would be quickly scorched out of existence.

That is part of the reason Uzziah's approach to the altar in the temple was such a serious matter. In his pride he had begun to think he was qualified to ascend to the level of God's throne.

The king was unconsciously assuming that his nature and God's were compatible. But the priests knew differently.

That they were privileged, unlike the king, to approach the altar where God's holiness was uniquely concentrated was a condescension on God's part. Priests were specially designated, by God's choice, to approach the heavenly Presence on behalf of all others—even a proud king. Uzziah's leprosy was a sign of what happens to one who presumes on this delicate act of grace.

The judgment of Uzziah and the contrasting holiness of God ought to give the contemporary worshiper much thought when he or she enters into the presence of God in worship. Are we much too flippant in those moments when we exalt him and offer up our devotion?

The second part of the liturgy of the seraphim is of

equal importance, ". . . the whole earth is full of his glory. . . ." Within this second line of the heavenly hymn is a further insight as to why Isaiah became a changed man. For the first time he caught a glimpse of the glory of God, a heavenly phenomena comparable, I suspect, to the rays of the sun which flood the earth. Glory is a radiating splendor of all that a holy God is; the earth is full of it. Full, perhaps, with the exception of the part of the earth which humanity has misused and polluted.

The contemplative wrestles with the issue of how to experience the glory of God. His or her spiritual disciplines are in part designed to open the pores of the inner spirit so that it might absorb all that God is willing to offer in revelation of himself. Anyone can tell who has returned to the north in the dead of winter after exposure to the beautiful Caribbean sun. Just so it is often possible to point out those who have been seeing glimpses of the glory of the heavenly King.

My thoughts spring back to Moses whose face was so brilliant with reflected glory after he had conversed with God on the holy mountain, that the Hebrew people petitioned him to veil his face when he addressed the tribes. Even this secondary source of God's glory was far too much for them to absorb at first glance.

What of those who resist the glory of God? I read of strange insects and fish living in deep caverns who, in all the generations of life, have never been exposed to sunlight. The biologist who studies them points to empty sockets where there were once eyes. Having no light, they need no eyes. They have adapted, the biologist says, to their environment.

The contemplative, having touched the glory of God, worries that his people may face the same experience. Should they choose to shield themselves from the glory of God, they will slowly lose their capacity to see the light of glory and, beyond that, see what the light of that glory reveals.

I become aware of this truth when I take a plane flight from Boston to Chicago for two days of meetings at the airport hotel. From my car in Boston, I walk to an elevator which brings me to the proper gate. I walk down a covered ramp and into a plane which is soon flying at an altitude of 37,000 feet. Again, an enclosed ramp aids me in leaving the plane. I walk the corridors of O'Hare airport, cross underneath the roadway through a tunnel, and enter a hotel which becomes a place for eating, sleeping, and meeting for two days. Never once do I leave the building, even when it comes time to walk through the tunnel, along the corridors, down another ramp and into a Boston-bound plane which returns me to my car. Throughout all of the forty-eight hours, I have never once been touched by the sun. I have breathed artificially cooled air; I have surrounded myself with a manufactured environment.

Should I persist in living this way indefinitely, my skin would become pallid, my respiratory system could be adversely affected, and I would probably face some emotional reactions. In adapting to living without the sun, I would become less and less fully human.

Isaiah's generation was busy cutting off the "sun" of the glory of God. Again and again as he would see the evidences of that happening, he would be reminded of the affirmations of the seraphim. "The whole earth is full of God's glory. . . ." It is a great fact that is unnoticed by those who have attempted to insulate themselves from it. Paul would later describe them as ". . . those who suppress the truth . . . changing the glory of the immortal God for images resembling mortal man or birds or animals or reptiles."

Isaiah is lost for adequate descriptors when he goes on to record the result of this liturgy: "And the foundations of the thresholds shook at the voice of him who called, and the house was filled with smoke" (Isa. 6:3).

Did anyone in the crowd listening to Isaiah's story of this vision pick up the irony of shaking foundations—especially those around the thresholds—in a temple as substantial as Jerusalem? It was inconceivable that any power could shake Solomon's Temple. It doesn't matter whether this is a visionary temple or the real one. The fact that it shook to the foundations is cause for alarm, and it bespeaks something of the great power that is involved in this worship of a holy and glorious God. The contemplative understands that.

The cloud of smoke is perhaps too much of a mystery to confidently nail down to a clear understanding. It could be that which results from the burning of incense, a sign of divine presence. Or it could be the vapors which arise when cold meets hot, and unrighteousness meets righteousness.

There is no doubt, however, that this had been an impressionable experience for the contemplative Isaiah. In this experience he had taken a giant leap forward toward seeing reality not just in terms of the world of Ahaz and Sargon, to name a few, but he had now added the dimension of a heavenly world where God's majesty and power are discerned. It almost always happens this way when someone sees the Lord.

It would appear that the modern exercises of personal faith have provided many with knowledge of God. But it is debatable whether many have *seen* God. Today there is a plethora of attractive and witty Christian leaders who have commandeered the Christian scene by way of the media and the various gadgets of communication. We are inundated with speculations about the future and systems of life in the present. Many even pay for the privilege of exposure to the learned ones aboard special cruises and tours. Tuition is charged and great halls and arenas are crowded by those desperate for answers to the complexities of life. But out of it all come few reports of anyone who, like Isaiah, has seen the Lord.

How can we hope as Christians to provide a sure and certain word to a drifting society of the turbulent eighties and nineties without the perspective of the ancient contemplative who saw the Lord? This is what A. W. Tozer was trying to tell us when he placed the first priority on how we see God:

The heaviest obligation lying upon the Christian church today is to purify and elevate her concept of God until it is once more worthy of Him—and of her. In all her prayers and labors this should have first place. We do the greatest service to the next generation of Christians by passing on to them undimmed and undiminished that noble concept of God which we received from our Hebrew and Christian fathers of generations past. This will prove of greater value to them than anything that art or science can devise. [*Knowledge of the Holy* (New York: Harper & Row, 1975, paper), p. 12]

We should not prematurely envy the contemplative who sees the Lord, however. We should not covet Isaiah's experience until we understand what it did to him. For there followed his sight of the Lord a highly focused sight of some other realities which he had not apparently seen with such clarity before. Much of that clarity was not pleasurable; it was painful, like a burst of light which hammers eyes that have been in the dark too long. Isaiah's vision was just getting started.

AXIOM TEN
A person for turbulent times possesses a keen self-awareness, displaying the fruits of brokenness and humility. Recognizing there is within him or her an instinctive proneness to sin, this person nurtures a healthy fear of offending a righteous God and, conversely, a delight in walking in the holy way.

12/ On seeing myself

In the room where I sit writing and rewriting these thoughts there are the notes of a magnificent symphony being played. There is also the captivating beat of a jazz combo, and the lilting voices of a chorale singing love songs. But I can hear none of them because right now they are merely in the form of radio waves to which I've not responded. I've turned off the stereo. Although I love music, I've chosen to reject it while I write so that my mind and spirit will be as alert as possible.

Whether or not I flip the switch that will make the music heard in the room makes no difference as to the music's presence. It plays on unheard even though I have chosen not to acknowledge it.

I may make a similar choice if the sun at the window makes the room too hot. I may draw the drapes. But the sun will still be out there projecting its rays at the window. I've simply chosen to resist its overpowering gifts of warmth.

Isaiah, given the opportunity, *chose* to see the Lord in his holiness and glory. He heard what the seraphim said to each other about the King. And because he saw and heard, he began to feel the effects of the vision. It is important to remember that the heavenly activity would have continued to happen, as it does to this day, even if Isaiah had chosen *not* to respond to it. Had he—by way of analogy—turned the switch of his spirit to the off position, or had he drawn the drapes over his inner being, the vision for him would have ended there and then. But he didn't! He chose to participate in the vision. Thus, he entered the track of contemplative worship.

And experience with God brings a mixture of reactions. Some of them are, of course, the feelings of ecstasy, for the beauty of God is something to cause spiritual exhilaration. But there is another reaction all too often ignored, one that seems to have been spiritually instinctive for Isaiah. Having seen the Lord, Isaiah saw himself. It was not the sight one sees when looking into a mirror. There a person sees shape, color, and orderliness or disorderliness.

Isaiah's sight of self was something like an X ray. It caused him to see for the first time the condition of his inner being. It revealed any debasing habit patterns, attitudes or values which had their origins there. It unveiled for him the state of his proximity to the Lord upon the throne. Apparently this was not a happy discovery.

The contemplative knows that the pursuit of God takes a form of courage, for he or she understands that while there is that exhilaration in the discovery of God, there is a certain pain as self is also exposed. The ache of self-exposure is nothing new. The first man, Adam, somehow sensed that, should God find him in the garden after he had disobeyed his law, there would be a sort of embarrassment as his shame was revealed. Thus he hid. He didn't want to see God because he didn't wish his own condition to be x-rayed.

There is an intriguing theme through Scripture which I call that of personal embarrassment. It is seen in its ultimate sense when Paul described a moment yet to

come when every person will stand before God with
"mouth stopped," having no excuse for choices made
that created a state of rebellion against God's laws.

That theme of embarrassment is seen again and again as
people come to grips with their condition and how far they
have fallen short of the glory of God. The prodigal son,
for example, reached a point of crushing embarrassment in a
pigsty when he "came to himself" and realized how badly
he had squandered both his father's love and resources.

A crowd confronted with the reality of their acts of
crucifying Christ were "cut to the heart" when they faced
up to the dimensions of their crime at Calvary. A jailer at
Philippi was constrained to cry out "What must I do?"
when he saw himself in the light of God's power in Paul's
life.

You could say that Isaiah was suddenly embarrassed in
much the same way, having tasted the glory of God. One of
the proofs that we have really come into God's presence
is our almost immediate sense of unworthiness, our
awareness that we are really much less than he originally
designed us to be as human beings.

Unlike Adam who fled to the bushes, Isaiah faced up to
the full fury of self-exposure:

And I said, "Woe is me! For I am lost; for I am a man of
unclean lips, and I dwell in the midst of a people of
unclean lips; for my eyes have seen the King, the Lord of
hosts!"

As Isaiah described his vision of the heavenly King, it
may be that the crowd moved closer to him with mounting
tension. This was fascinating indeed. Someone may have
asked, "And what did you say or do when you experienced
all of this?"

The dramatist in me suggests that Isaiah may have
stopped for a few seconds, gulped a bit and squinted eyes
he hoped would not fill with tears.

Then a response to the question. "For the first time I
began to see myself as I should have done a long time ago."
Imagine him going on to add, "You may think it offensive
for me to confront a king with his stupidity, with his

sinfulness. You may resent my denunciations of a city for its toleration of injustice. And you may not appreciate what drives me to question the motives and practices of our business people. But I want you to know that before I could ever say 'Woe!' to any of this, I had to say it first of myself. Remember! I had to say it first of myself."

The word *woe*, frequently used by prophets, is a word which means "imperfect, not complete." It describes something which is no longer what it was meant to be.

Many men and women of my congregation work in the great technical industries of the northeast. They are involved in the design and manufacture of micro-processors and forms of electronic circuitry so minute that the product can only be examined through the lenses of powerful microscopes. These people work with specifications which measure tolerances to within the closest millionth of an inch.

When one of these components made for a computer or a communications system is examined by the people in quality control and it fails to meet the design specifications (the specs, they call them), the product is returned either to be discarded or remade. If it has not met the demands of the specs, one could say of the component, "woe." And it could also be said that when quality control exposes the fault in a memorandum to the production line, it is crying, "woe!"

Having seen perfection in God, Isaiah immediately saw imperfection in himself. True worship of God, true assessment of self. Two factors necessary to the full-orbed worship experience.

Isaiah's analysis of what he saw in himself is impressive. He acknowledged first of all a "lost" condition. That results, he said, in personal actions which are less than admirable. Finally, he recognized that he was mutually culpable with everyone else for the unrighteous state of affairs within the society of Israel and Judah. This threefold awareness of genuine woefulness can give us a fairly complete idea of the nature of confession in the act of worship.

The act of confession is the unconditional

acknowledgment that the worshiper is not what God originally made him to be. In confession we face that sorrowful fact that we were born into an inherited condition of unrighteousness and that we have made choices with great frequency which have caused us to drift from the fellowship and blessing of the God who has made us for himself.

Out of all of this has come an equal drift from other human beings, for when we are "lost" from God, we are actually "lost" from each other. Compared to what God meant all relationships to be, when we are lost from each other, the truth is that we hardly know each other. In confession we face all of this and finally conclude, like Isaiah did, that we are indeed co-conspirators with all others in the downward spiral that takes all of creation away from God. "I dwell in the midst of an unclean people. . . ."

William Barclay refers to a letter by the Puritan preacher, Thomas Goodwin, written to his son in which he writes:

When I was threatening to become cold in my ministry, and when I felt the Sabbath morning coming, and my heart not filled with amazement at the grace of God, or when I was making ready to dispense the Lord's Supper, do you know what I used to do? I used to take a turn up and down among the sins of my past life, and I always came down with a broken and contrite heart, ready to preach, as it was preached in the beginning, the forgiveness of sins.

Later he went on to write:

Many a Sabbath morning, when my soul had been cold and dry for the lack of prayer during the week, a turn up and down in my past life before I went into the pulpit always broke my heart, and made me close with the gospel for my own soul before I began to preach.

A contemplative understands this sort of thinking and accepts it. It is a part of worship that cannot be avoided, although there may be many who try. No one can worship behind Adam's bushes. Therefore, part of the contemplative's liturgy is the seeking out of further insight

into the status of one's personal and spiritual condition. It
must be known so that it can be dealt with, and healed.

It strikes me that I am Adam. I am among those who
are momentarily comforted in the protection of the bushes. I
must discipline myself with daily regularity to face the
woefulness of my inner self. If I avoid this exercise, the
alternative is an increasing ignorance of the inner
espionage activity which is slowly strangling my spirit.
Resisting the humbling experience of confession, I must
summon up greater and greater energy from other sources
to fight tendencies and habit patterns which are an
embarrassment to me and those about me.

Elizabeth O'Connor perceives this when she writes:

Meditation and confession are ways of firmly
establishing in consciousness, and thus in the storehouse of
the brain, other facts that will help the new in us do
battle with the old. Often we try to change something in
ourselves by violent combat with it. Even when we are
successful, keeping vigil over the vanquished enemy
requires all kinds of energy. We dare not expose ourselves
to anything which might threaten the position we have
obtained by much sacrifice. Our attitude toward life
becomes unyielding and defensive, so uneasy is the peace
that we have made within, and so uncertain are we as to
when we might have to make war again. . . . The "evil urge"
in us that we acknowledge and call by name is deprived
by that act of its power to control our life and destiny.
[*Search for Silence* (Waco, TX: Word, 1973), p. 43]

The contemplative is not depressed at the daily
discovery of repetitive or previously unknown pockets of
spiritual rebellion or disorderliness. He or she knows that
the closer one draws to the source of light, the deeper and
more marked are the shadows. Such awareness of self,
therefore, is a sign that there has been an awareness of God.

Isaiah's confession is offered on three levels. There was
first a consistent acknowledgment of the spiritual disease
called sin. This very assertion is a wound to human
pride.

Acknowledging ourselves to have such a moral disease can be illustrated in the act in which a patient faces the evidences of a cancer that the physician has discovered. There can only be successful treatment if the patient will approach the physician at the time of his appointments with a consistent awareness that he is sick and in need of assistance. If the physician must repersuade him during every examination, or—worse yet—if the patient intermittently goes to great length to deny the existence of the cancer, can there be any worthwhile treatment at all? And of course, what if the patient should fail even to appear for the appointment?

Isaiah's statement, "I am lost . . ." is his signal that he knows of a condition within himself that, if left untreated, will render him ineffective to live in the heavenly world and, progressively, in the earthly world. Every contemplative exercise in which the gates of his heart are opened to God must be accompanied by a reaffirmation of his own lostness apart from the saving grace of God.

Peter's act of falling before Jesus Christ following the miracle of the fish-filled nets and saying "Depart from me, O Lord, for I am a sinful man . . ." is parallel to Isaiah's words, "I am lost." In observing the power of the miracle, Peter has sensed something of the heavenly nature of Jesus. That glimpse of Jesus was powerful enough to force him into the sight of his inner self which was not attractive.

Credit Peter with the honesty to express his struggle. What he saw of himself in contrast to the powerful Christ was so distressing that he thought himself incapable of overcoming the gap that separated them.

How beautiful, therefore, the words of Jesus who looked at Peter and in response to his confession simply said, "Don't be afraid . . . for henceforth you will be fishing for men." In a sentence Jesus put the fearful Peter at his ease. That which the fisherman lacked, Jesus would complete. That is the grace which brings to the confession of the contemplative the acts of forgiveness and a commencement of the process of eternal salvation.

That second confession of Isaiah the contemplative is a

more specific and systematic look at the specific sins in
daily life. It is a sorrowful rehearsal of attitudes, actions,
and propensities which are spiritually and morally
destructive, those things which create an ever-widening
gap between persons and their God. For Isaiah it was, "I am
a man of unclean lips," something many of us might also
find it necessary to admit.

In a society which has moved increasingly toward the
secular, the emphasis has been to downgrade if not
obliterate any talk of sin or sins. Some have pointed out
that attention given to sins is "guilt-producing," and guilt is
at the root of many mental and emotional problems. It
has been suggested, therefore, that we eliminate guilt, and
the simple method for doing that is to do away with
anything originally called sin. In other words, if a troubled
person visits a counselor who in turn diagnoses the
problem as stemming from the guilt raised by an act of
marital infidelity, why not convince the client that there was
nothing wrong with the infidelity? If there is no sin, there is
no guilt. Satisfaction guaranteed.

This in fact can be done *if* there is no God whose nature
is holy and who calls upon us to respond to his glory. *If*
there is no God who determines what sin is, then it will
be left to the human race to determine what sin may be.
Should that be the case, humanity will determine sin by
majority vote or by taking a survey. In societies marked with
totalitarian regimes, sin will no doubt be determined by
those in power.

But Isaiah saw the Lord. And in seeing him, he was
brought to full attention concerning those acts which the
Lord had called offensive. In the context of this vision, he
became specifically mindful that his lips ought to be covered
because they were not in the habit of saying those things
which met with God's standards.

Isaiah's concept of unclean lips is difficult to pin down
any further than this. It may be that he sees his speaking as
in sharp contrast with what the seraphim were saying. He
began to realize that it had been a long time if ever since he
had acknowledged God in the way the seraphim spoke.
He is obviously unworthy to join their song.

The more obvious interpretation of Isaiah's thought is

that he realized that he had great persuasive and oratorical power and that he had used it irresponsibly. Now in this moment it was becoming clear to him that he had misused the gift of God in his life.

A more subtle aspect of this confession might have something to do with Isaiah's previous reluctance to speak out about what sin was in the community. We have no way of knowing what Isaiah's role in the community was before the vision. He could easily have been a member of the priestly household or held some leadership function. It may be that he was suddenly shocked with how easy it had been for him to comply in silence with the things that were going on about him. To remain silent and not use his voice for the interests of God was really to have had lips that were in fact unclean.

Although I have enjoyed a strongly supportive marriage with my wife, Gail, there have been a few minor irritants which we have failed to resolve in the years of our relationship. Among them has been our constant disagreement while driving our car in the rain as to how spotted the windshield must be before the driver turns on the wipers. I for one can tolerate a rain-spotted windshield just a bit longer than Gail can. The span between our tolerances inevitably generates a conversation which sounds like, "I can't see a thing. Why must I always ask you to turn the wipers on?" To which I respond, "I can see perfectly; the wipers are too distracting."

Confession of our sins means that we seek to wipe our spirits clean. It conveys to God our concern that nothing spot the surface of our spirits that would make the sight of him difficult. The contemplative does not have a high tolerance for the "spotted" windshield of the spirit. He or she knows that when it is left unwiped that the sight of both heaven and earth becomes difficult at best. Uncleaned spirits leave us vulnerable to situations in which increasing numbers of decisions can be made which are insensitive and often ignorant, gathering consequences as time passes that we really do not want to live with.

Why are many of us not alarmed over the fact that millions "worship" each week but never are confronted with the need to wipe the windshield clean? Worship

becomes an art form, the pursuit of religious beauty. It
becomes something of an evangelistic service in which the
success of the act is measured in terms of how many
people respond to an invitation. Or worship becomes the
pursuit of personal inspiration, something to make us
feel good, to be at ease with ourselves, God, and each other.
But rarely are people encouraged to do face to face battle
with their sins.

The third phase of Isaiah's confession is of equal
performance. It is an important insight—understood by the
contemplative—but often overlooked by the Christian
marked by Western culture. Isaiah acknowledges, "I dwell
in the midst of a people of unclean lips."

Isaiah has come to grips with the fact that sin is not
entirely an individual act. There is a mystical
sense—certainly very real to God—in which we
participate in one another's sins, both cause and effect.
Isaiah seems to be recognizing that the sins of his
countrymen have affected him. But he is also
acknowledging that in part their sins are his also.

A few years ago I stood before a shrine erected in
Manila in memory of the atrocities committed by Japanese
soldiers against Filipino and American prisoners of war.
Beside me was a friend, a pastor from Japan. Together we
had come to the Philippines to speak to a number of
Christian congregations. As we stood there reading the
inscriptions of the monuments I noticed my friend begin
to weep.

"Why do you weep?" I asked.

My friend responded, "I am weeping because of this great
sin. I weep because of the guilt of it. I am so sorry."

"But," I protested, "you did not do this. We were
newborn babies when this happened. There is nothing
for you to feel sorry for."

"No," he said, "I was not here, but my countrymen
were here, and what they did is my sin also. I share in the
guilt of it."

I was deeply affected by this perspective of a Christian
from an oriental culture. It had not occurred to me ever to
repent of the atrocities that some of the American soldiers

committed in Vietnam. That had been someone else's sin, certainly not mine.

But I was wrong. The oriental Christian understands something the Westerner might find hard to grasp; that there is responsibility for the sins of a culture which we must all share. And part of confession is that act of acknowledging our complicity in a land where we dwell with people of unclean lips. Confession for the contemplative does not remove him from the flux and flow of the world about, but it in ract may inject him even more deeply into it. First, because he's part of it; secondly, because he becomes now all the more responsible for it.

It becomes clear now why so many of the prayers of God's people resound with phrases like "I and my fathers have sinned." It is also clear how dangerous the state is of that brand of Christianity which eschews confessional responsibility for the world's plight. It is relatively easy to say, "The world must be evangelized and saved from its sins." It is much more difficult to say, "We are the world and we are part of the reason why it must be saved from its sins. We have bombed; we have tortured; we have oppressed; we have stolen; we have exploited."

Confession for the contemplative is painful. It is a new effort every day and few there are who wish to get this serious about it.

In the *Genesse Diary*, Henri Nouwen tells of a day when he was assigned to work with two other Trappist monks in the monastery's bakery. As they worked side by side preparing the raisin bread for baking, suddenly one of the brothers stopped the machine which washed the raisins and indicated that he was aware that a stone had just passed through with the raisins into the tub where raisins were prepared to be mixed in with the dough of the bread.

Nouwen was incredulous! "How could you hear one tiny stone in the midst of all these millions of raisins?" he asked. The Trappist brother simply responded, "I just hear it," and he added, "we have to find that stone. If a lady gets it in her bread, she can break her tooth on it and we could be sued." Nouwen went on to write, that pointing to a large bathtub-like container full of washed raisins the

Trappist brother said, "We have to push those through again until we find that stone."

Nouwen writes, "I couldn't believe it. Brother Benedict hadn't been able to detect the stone while the raisins came out, but Brother Theodore was so sure that objection was senseless. Millions of raisins went through again, and just when I'd given up ever finding that stone—it seemed like looking for a needle in a haystack—something clicked. 'There it is,' Theodore said. 'It jumped against the metal wall of the washer.' Benedict looked carefully and moved his hands through the last ounce of raisins. There it was! A small purple-blue stone, just as large as a raisin. Theodore took it and gave it to me with a big smile."

Nouwen concludes his remembrance of this event in this way:

In a strange way this even meant a lot to me. Yesterday I was carrying granite rocks out of the river. Today we were looking for a small stone among millions of raisins. I was impressed, not only by Theodore's alertness, but even more by his determination to find it and take no risks. He really is a careful diagnostician. This little stone could have harmed someone—a lady or a monastery. [*Genesse Diary* (Garden Grove, NY: Doubleday, 1976), pp. 16, 17]

Nouwen's parable of the stone is parallel with Isaiah's experience in the visionary temple. One cannot see God without becoming aware of the stones in one's life. In the face of his righteousness and holiness, in the midst of the experience of the worship of the heavenly family, we begin to see ourselves. We see ourselves in different ways; perhaps in the same three ways as Isaiah saw himself: his own condition of sinfulness, his sinful acts, and his complicity in the world situation.

Should there be contemporary contemplatives this is where they will come from: the closet in which confession is made to a holy God. There is no other route worth even thinking about. Such people are humble, contrite, malleable to the Spirit of God. We desperately need some people like that today.

AXIOM ELEVEN
A person for turbulent times drinks deeply from the fountain of the grace of God, who desires that all might be liberated from the suffocation of guilt and regret. Living in grace, the person for turbulent times speaks gladly of a free spirit and an expanding mind.

13/ The liberation of a contemplative

Somewhere out of the Vietnam war came the account of a news correspondent who spent a day in a field hospital. His attention became riveted upon an army nurse whose uniform was drenched with blood and whose face showed the marks of painful fatigue. Watching her work over the broken bodies of wounded soldiers, he finally remarked to her, "I wouldn't do what you're doing for a million dollars." And her answer: "Brother, neither would I."

What makes people step out of the flow of convenience, comfort, and security to do the hard thing? That question has been pondered by many preachers and leaders whose responsibility it has been to challenge people to ministry. All too often people are recruited on one of two superficial and inauthentic bases.

A. W. Tozer spoke to the first of the two when he wrote:

Probably the hardest thought of all for our natural egotism
to entertain is that God does not need our help. We
commonly represent him as a busy, eager, somewhat
frustrated father hurrying about seeking help to carry out
his benevolent plan to bring peace and salvation to the
world. . . . The God who worketh all things surely needs
no help and no helpers.

Too many missionary appeals are based upon this
fancied frustration of Almighty God. An effective speaker
can easily excite pity in his hearers not only for the
heathen but for the God who has tried so hard and so long to
save them and has failed for want of support. I fear that
thousands of young persons enter Christian service from
no higher motive than to help deliver God from the
embarrassing situation his love has gotten him into and his
limited abilities seem unable to get him out of. Add to
this a certain degree of commendable idealism and a fair
amount of compassion for the underprivileged and you
have the true drive behind much Christian activity today.

Again, God needs no defenders. He is the Eternal
Undefended. [Tozer, *Knowledge of the Holy*, p. 41]

Tozer was very blunt. His God was so great that he
couldn't imagine the puny view most of us have
inadvertently entertained. You can be sure that Isaiah's
view of God was just as great if not greater. He would
never have been impressed with a motivation to serve based
on the notion that God was in deep trouble.

A second and often-used motivator is pure emotion. Tell
stories; quote overwhelming amounts of statistics; raise
guilt; thrill hearts! It's an unbeatable combination of events
that will pull people forward, willing to do anything: go,
give, pray—usually for not more than a few weeks.

You and I will never produce or even be Isaiah-types
based upon a limited view of God or the strength of an
emotional appeal. And yet that is exactly what people
often do with the words of Isaiah in the account we have
examined when they speak to the text, "Here am I; send
me!"

It is a dramatic and lovely phrase, and set off by itself, it is guaranteed to excite the sensitivities of some. But not usually for long.

It is important to examine the content of the context and see that Isaiah's willingness to affirm that he was ready to be sent into a very ugly world is based upon an earlier experience of inner liberation. That is something all too frequently overlooked.

My neighbor enjoys the luxury of a radio-controlled garage door. I watch him gloat just a bit as he swings his automobile into the driveway, presses a button on a tiny instrument in his car, and sees the garage door spring upward. Inside of his garage is a mechanism tuned to respond to a certain coded signal. And when it hears the signal activated by my neighbor, it does its work.

In creation human beings were made with a mechanism that would respond to the signals of God. In Eden where God sought the company of Adam and Eve, he called. Their pure hearts were programmed to respond to the signal, and the fellowship of God and persons was sweet.

One day my neighbor expressed some frustration because his garage door began to go up and down even though he hadn't sent the signal. Now it was my turn to gloat and affirm, in a kidding way of course, that technology was failing again. What activated the motor? Weeks later we learned that a satellite orbiting overhead several thousand miles in space was sending signals on the same frequency, and each time it passed overhead it managed to convey the false message to my neighbor's garage door that it was time to open.

False signals can be a real problem. The Genesis account describes how the serpent counterfeited the signals of God and goaded the first man and woman into decisions and actions which were increasingly resistant to God's call for fellowship. The first time God came to speak to them after the serpent's visit, they resisted him due to their embarrassment and unwillingness to account for what had happened. And then, more and more, it became their habit to resist God's ways, choosing alternatives that were a consistent disappointment to their Maker.

You can see a good example of God sending signals both

of love and warning when he reminded Cain that his
pattern of resistance was going to get him into deep
trouble. But Cain refused to respond and his life spiralled
downhill toward disaster.

Back to Isaiah. The prophet's contemplative experience
in the "temple" caused his heart to respond to God's
signal. But the response was not that of emotion or the desire
to be a hero, to help God out. It was because his heart was
liberated to be a heart once again, to hear what God was
saying. And what was it that caused the liberation? A
healing experience which followed hard on the steps of his
confession.

As the confession was threefold, so was the response. You
can picture Isaiah trying to share this part of his vision
with the crowd gathered to hear him that wanted an
explanation of his prophetic origins.

Then flew one of the seraphim to me, having in his hand
a burning coal which he had taken with tongs from the altar.
And he touched my mouth, and said: "Behold, this has
touched your lips; your guilt is taken away, and your sin is
forgiven."

This act of cleansing seems to bypass the normal
procedures used by people of Isaiah's day to pursue
atonement for their sins. Isaiah brings no lamb or
appropriate offering. In fact, "nothing in his hands he
brings." He can only offer his honest acknowledgment of
his condition and his personal sense of unworthiness.

Isaiah must have done something right, however,
because his confession touched off an act by the seraphim
which resulted in Isaiah's forgiveness. The fact is that
Isaiah's experience is one taught in the New Testament.
Forgiveness is an act of grace and response to confession,
John wrote (1 John 1:9). And John could say that looking back
upon the ultimate sacrifice of Christ upon the cross.

What sacrifice is there in Isaiah's vision? Could it be that
the burning coals on the altar inform us that there is
perpetual sacrifice, the benefits of which are reaching out to
Isaiah through the touch by the angel? In fact, does this
particular vision really situate itself in a timeless context
so that—mysterious as it seems—Isaiah was forgiven

through the grace extended in the sacrifice at Calvary by Christ? Though we know the cross to have been at a certain date in time and space, we are seeing here the cross in its timeless reality. Isaiah is forgiven *now* through the effects of something yet to come; yet it is as if it had already happened. Such is the reality in the heavenly presence where all things are in the eternal now.

The coal burns but is carried by tongs where it is applied to Isaiah's lips. He made no comment about pain, only about the words of the one who applied it: "guilt is taken away; sin forgiven."

The first statement speaks to Isaiah's spiritual condition. Surgery had been done upon the spiritual cancer. The guilt had been taken away. He needed no longer be embarrassed; he was free to join the heavenly chorus who call to one another. He was in effect one of them.

His sin was forgiven. The acts of his unclean lips had been atoned for. Now he was free to use the lips in a positive service for the King. They were usable now for constructive matters. The man was free to be and to act. He was liberated.

We must not overlook this encounter that Isaiah reported he had with one of the seraphim. It seems to be a great line of demarcation between the past and the future in Isaiah's life. From this point everything seemed to change. From henceforth Isaiah would think with a different perspective and speak with a different message. He would never be the same again.

We must learn two things from this experience. One is the necessity of that initial moment where a person chooses to let God confront him with himself. Perhaps it will never be as dramatic a moment as the one Isaiah has shared. But we must seek the sight of him nevertheless. Christians testify that this happens as we meet the Jesus Christ of history. "No one has ever seen God; the only Son, who is in the bosom of the Father, he has revealed him" (John 1:18). Jesus himself would later say, "I am the way, and the truth, and the life; no one comes to the Father but by me" (John 14:6).

We can also deduce from Isaiah's experience that formation it gives us for each daily experience in the

presence of God. There is an outline here for the pattern
of contemplative worship which brings us to the altar
upon which there is an adequate cleansing experience for
each one who comes with the same "nothing" that Isaiah
brought with him.

Paul Rees tells of discovering among his late father's
personal effects a memo describing an experience with
God:

The solitude of this small study is more to my poor soul
than all of my social intercourse with humanity. It is
here that I am transported to the sunlit peaks where eternal
verities blaze and glow in unfading splendor, until all that
is terrestial passes into eclipse.

Amid misunderstandings, period, toil, and pain, an
hour with Him behind these four walls reveals the Great
White Way and lends the strength to climb Heaven's
steepest ascents. What strange strength I derive in this
solitary nook.

The Jewish theologian, Abraham Joshua Heschel,
understood this experience of the contemplative seeking
God's presence.

I should like to stress that acts that occur within the
inner life of man, a thought, a moment of sensitivity, a
moment of stillness, and self-examination, the
acquistion of a spiritual insight, this is supremely practical.
[*Insecurity of Freedom* (New York: Schocken, 1972), p. 50]

But Isaiah's liberation statement is not ended. The
third aspect of his liberation was the result of the first two.
Isaiah was now liberated for the first time to hear the
voice of God speaking heavenly secrets.

Isaiah had not spoken of the voice of God before this
moment. It would appear that he simply hadn't heard it
until now. Before the vision occurred, Isaiah was caught up
in hearing the voices of the world about him. He was
caught up with the sound of his own voice, I suppose. But
now for the first time, having been liberated in terms of his
spiritual condition and patterns of action, Isaiah was

tuned in on God's signal. He sensed God's concerns; he
responded to God's ways.

Perhaps that was what Thomas a Kempis was getting at
when he wrote:

For when the grace of God comes to a man, then he is
able to do all things. And when it leaves him, then he
becomes poor and weak, and seems reserved only for
chastisement. At such times you must not be cast down or
give away to depression, but be conformed to the will of
God, and bear calmly whatever may come upon you for the
glory of Jesus Christ; for after winter comes the summer,
after night the day, after the storm the quiet calm.

What was it that Isaiah heard? God saying, "Whom shall I
send? Who will go for us?" It was an invitation. The
conclusion of worship actually. That moment when the
contemplative, having adored the Being of God and
having experienced his own cleansing, could now respond to
the heart of God. Even as worship should never cease
without the call to confession, worship should never cease
until the contemplative has seen how to respond to what
is experienced. For the first time Isaiah was aware that God
had a message for the people of his land. He was inviting
Isaiah to deliver it. And out of gratitude, Isaiah was only
too glad to offer himself.

The third aspect of Isaiah's liberation was the privilege of
hearing God's voice and responding to his invitation to
serve. From what had Isaiah been liberated? From a narrow
view of history. From a blindness to the consequences of
man's prevailing choices. From a destiny spent in the
pursuit of things which would not count or last. From a
stifling perspective limited to the brainpower of the kings
and princes of the times who were making colossal
errors. From his own habitual tendencies of spiritual
shortsightedness which were a detriment to himself and
those about him. From deafness and blindness which had
inhibited from knowing heretofore about the God who
seeks the wholeness of the humanity he created.

Following the death of the singer Elvis Presley there
arose an enormous number of people around the world who

were prepared to do anything to affirm their allegiance to the dead singer. Among the most fanatical was Dennis Wise who had collected memorabilia about Presley since he was a small child. Throughout his school years, Dennis Wise had worn clothes like Presley, acted like Presley, and sought whatever proximity he could achieve to Presley. He acknowledged that he had been laughed at by schoolmates and teachers alike. He admitted that his preoccupation had cost him scholastic excellence.

After the rock singer died, Dennis Wise paid several thousand dollars to undergo a facial modification by a plastic surgeon in order to look like Elvis Presley. He came out of the operation as a reasonable facsimile.

Did Presley ever know while alive that Dennis Wise existed? "I never met him," Wise told reporters. "Once I stood on the wall of Graceland mansion and I saw him at a distance. I went to a few of his concerts. But, no, I never met him."

These are the things a human being might do to pursue a god. But Dennis Wise did them to pursue a man who he apparently thought to be a god. There is no liberation here. Nor is there anything of the personal touch experienced by Isaiah. There is nothing that brings much more than a lot of regrets, and might-have-beens.

But our God knows of our existence—each one of us. Christ went to great lengths to affirm that the smallest and the slightest of us were targets of God's love and of his call. Signals are sent but not always heard. Liberation must come first, and that is achieved by those who stand not out beyond the walls but those who come forth to the altar just as they are.

The failure of many to receive the signals of God, to hear his voice, results from all too many who think they have worshiped but really haven't. Until there is that moment of "woe," until there is that acknowledgment of continued embarrassment, there can be no flaming coal, no liberation, no moment of hearing the signal sent. And that is a major reason why there are few contemplatives today, and therefore, so few persons prepared for turbulent times.

AXIOM TWELVE
A person for turbulent times is not stunned into inaction when living
with the consequences created by the choices of a rebellious
generation. This person is rather saturated in hope, an optimism
that rejoices in the evidences of God's liberating grace at work.
When others are paralyzed and demoralized, this person brings into
the turbulence a deed of mercy and a world of joy.

14/ The contemplative's great idea

Our beloved New England is marked with scores of prep
schools which maintain the traditional ways for which
stolid New Englanders are noted. In one such New
Hampshire school years ago, the son of a wealthy Boston
businessman was suspended due to mischievous behavior.
As the story is related to me, his father, a prominent
member of the schoolboard, took the first train
northward to the campus and, after being announced,
stormed into the headmaster's office. His opening salvo at
the seated old man was hardly calculated to gain a
favorable resolution to the problem. "You damn well
think you're running this school all by yourself don't you?"

The headmaster stood slowly, looped his thumbs into
the pockets of his vest and said, in that flat tonal accent
that is indigenous to America's northeast: "Your
language is *koss* (coarse); your "gramma" is despicable; BUT
(now waving a finger) YOU HAVE GRASPED THE
I-DEE-AH."

To grasp the idea! That was what Isaiah's vision was all about: to see God as he should be seen, to see himself and his spiritual needs and find himself renewed and personally cleansed. But beyond that: to grasp a new idea of the world in which he lived, to see it for the first time not as the majority of the people saw it but as God saw it. And to speak forcefully from that perspective.

The contemplative has a different idea. Out of that idea comes new measurements, new dimensions, new conclusions about reality. This is what flows from the exchange of words. God: "Who will go for us?" Isaiah: "Here am I; send me."

Isaiah was willing to go because he had something new to talk about. It flowed from the authority of having been with God, of realizing the true nature of spiritual deadness, and of experiencing what true liberation of the spirit is all about. No wonder he was willing to go.

There is an additional dimension about contemplative faith that needs to be considered and is all too often ignored. That is simply the fact that the contemplative is finally a communicator. This is quite in contrast with the many who imply that the contemplative withdraws from everything and simply sits and perceives. Too many of the religious experiences of our day are simply calculated to reward a person with happiness, spiritual security, or a feeling of personal superiority. This can be true among evangelical Christians who pride themselves in a never-ending quest for spiritual growth. Contemplation for the sheer sake of contemplation or growth for the sake of growth is inadequate, dangerous, and selfish. But in contrast is one being equipped to reflect God's majesty and serve those around him, which is the real purpose of maturing and being more spiritually sensitive.

God would not allow the vision in the temple to be finished with Isaiah's personal renewal. Now there was business to discuss. A turbulent world had to be encountered, and Isaiah was the man for the hour. He had grasped the idea; now he must communicate it. In other words, he could not stay in the glorious atmosphere of the temple any more than Peter, James, or John could have

stayed on their mountain the day that Christ was
transfigured. There was a valley below, a world beyond
the front door. There an idea had to be communicated and
acted out.

When Anne Morrow Lindberg reflected upon her time of
retreat at a beach where there had been an idyllic
experience of personal tranquility, she flirted with the
notion that she ought not to return to the real world back
at home. She confided to her journal,

Total retirement is not possible. I cannot shed my
responsibility. I cannot permanently inhabit a desert
island. I cannot be a nun in the midst of family life. I would
not want to be. The solution for me, surely is in neither
total renunciation of the world, nor in total acceptance of it.
I must find a balance somewhere, or an alternating
rhythm between these two extremes; a swinging pendulum
between solitude and communion, between retreat and
return. In my periods of retreat, perhaps I can learn
something to carry back into my worldly life.

Now Isaiah must return to his worldly life but with a
new idea that would draw some and offend many others. But
return he must whatever the results. And as he looked at
the affairs of each day and watched the movements of those
in positions to make choices, he would of necessity have
to speak and reflect conclusions and concerns that many
would find unpopular.

His role would be threefold: he would *comment* upon
the events of his time, bringing to bear observations and
evaluations which would probably be heard from no other
person. Second, he would *confront* those who chose to
be at odds with God's ways. At such moments, his words
might be harsh and punishing, but barbed with prophetic
truth. Third, as God's spokesman, the contemplative
prophet would communicate *comfort* to those living
through the consequences of national and personal
choices. He would be the spokesman for new days and
new opportunities. And in this third role, he would be the
bearer of words that promised eventual peace and
restoration.

In the historical perspective we now can appreciate what it was that Isaiah was offering himself to do. His lot was to join a train of select men and women, all previously liberated, who would seem to have launched out on a repeatedly unsuccessful mission:

The Lord, the God of their fathers, sent persistently to them by his messengers, because he had compassion on his people and on his dwelling place; but they kept mocking the messengers of God, despising his words, and scoffing at his prophets, till the wrath of the Lord rose up against his people, till there was no remedy. [2 Chron. 36:15, 16]

Isaiah, the commentator, the confronter, the comforter. It was a strange affair to be cast in such a role and it was not too promising a start when he was commissioned with words such as these:

Go and say to this people: 'Hear and hear, but do not understand; see and see, but do not perceive.' Make the heart of this people fat, and their ears heavy, and shut their eyes; lest they see with their eyes, and hear with their ears, and understand with their hearts, and turn and be healed. [Isa. 6:9, 10]

"Frankly, Isaiah, you are going to preach and not be heard, you are going to warn and not be heeded." It is obvious that Isaiah was being promised very little success in his life as a prophet and contemplative communicator.

There are some, claiming Christian faith, who would—even though they might deny it—enjoy this special moment. Their practical hatred of things in the world causes them inner glee each time the effects of spiritual rebellion are felt in this age. Each disaster, each collapse, each crime wave, each outbreak of riot, war, or social disintegration is only further evidence that they are right while others are wrong. For some this is a moment to be savored, this moment of proof. But for Isaiah, it was a moment of grief. These are *his* people of whom God was speaking.

It is a grieved prophet, therefore, who cries out "O Lord, how long (must this sort of thing go on)?" How long must I preach like that? How long will this "jamming" of people's minds and hearts continue? How long will you allow people to live in such darkness?

Perhaps Isaiah should not have asked. The answer was painful:

Until cities lie waste without inhabitant, and houses without men, and the land is utterly desolate, and the Lord removes men far away, and the forsaken places are many in the midst of the land. And though a tenth remain in it, it will be burned again, like a terebinth or an oak, whose stump remains standing when it is felled. [Isa. 6:11-13]

How can a person live with a message like this? Does Isaiah have something in common with the physician who knows that his or her patient has a terminal illness? Is his only hope that of achieving some type of temporary remission before the final effects of the disease take place? God had decreed the judgment of the "holy" race: its cities leveled, its people removed and exiled. Is this all that Isaiah could take away from the altar to communicate to his world?

No, wait! There is something else! The stump (Isa. 6:13). Rivet your eye upon the stump, Isaiah suddenly said. Reaching back into some insight he suddenly declared as the vision concluded: "The holy seed is its stump!"

There is the conclusion of the matter. There was Isaiah's hope. For while there was death and destruction, there is going to be eventual resurrection. The stump was going to be the source of a new holy "land," a new holy "people." God had not abandoned his chosen race; there will be a resurrection in response to his unbreakable promises. That would keep Isaiah alive throughout the tragedy of the coming years.

I have been repeatedly amazed at how resilient are the tree stumps I've tried to cut out at Peace Ledge, our family retreat in New Hampshire. When I go out to cut down trees for winter fuel, my wife, Gail, inevitably reminds me to cut close to the ground. "Remember," she always says, "they'll get new growth next year if you don't cut them close." She's right, and when I ignore her I find that within a year there may be several shoots sprouting from the sides of the stump—some of them six to seven feet in height.

In this grim vision of a scorched land which was nothing but ruins and silence Isaiah saw the stump, the remains of something which was once towering and mighty and Isaiah knew what I've learned at Peace Ledge: the stump will sprout again; it can be depended upon. He would go back to his first world, the real world, with this difficult commission. He would say what had to be said and accept the reactions of the people. He would comment, he would confront, and he would comfort, but in the back of his mind every moment there would be the sight of that stump. What must be purged would live again.

In the year that King Uzziah died, a people—the majority—saw nothing but grief and despair. They were preoccupied with the present disaster. But in that same year one man saw the Lord, and when he returned from his experience, the people quickly began to learn that that meant that there were two ways of interpreting events. Isaiah marched into the worlds of three successive kings in Jerusalem and a swirl of national intrigue. As he walked the streets of God's city, he saw the movements of the rich and the poor, of the religious establishment, of those in commerce. He was indeed a person for turbulent times.

As the years wore on there were many people who wished they had never seen this man. He had an irritating way of speaking in broad generalities. He would seize on what seemed to be trivia and amplify it to exorbitant proportions. Conversely, he had a habit of scoffing at the significance of those things which terrified the knowledgeable or delighted those pursuing security. It seemed as if Isaiah was always out of step with what the majority thought. Perhaps that was what A. W. Tozer meant when he wrote:

The moment we make up our minds that we are going on with this determination to exalt God over all, we step out of the world's parade. We shall find ourselves out of adjustment to the ways of the world, and increasingly so as we make progress in the holy way. We shall acquire a new viewpoint; a new and different psychology will be formed within us; a new power will begin to surprise us by its upsurgings and its outgoings. [*Pursuit of God* (Harrisburg, PA: Christian Publications, 1948)]

Isaiah the contemplative had grasped the idea and he set out from the site of that visionary encounter with God to comment, to confront, and to comfort. His turbulent world and ours are not unalike, and thus it is obvious that we need his vision, his insight, and his message.

AXIOM THIRTEEN
A person for turbulent times owns an eternal measurement by which to certify the true meaning of success and failure, security and vulnerability, beauty and ugliness. This person is unafraid to give a minority report. This person can expect to be ignored in the first phases of decision-making, but will usually be consulted when catastrophe lurks on the horizon.

15/ Isaiah, the commentator

A friend of mine shared with me the story of a young music student who strolled into the music studio of his piano instructor, asking somewhat glibly, "What's the news?"

The professor seized his tuning fork, struck it on a hard edge, and held it up so that the clear vibrating tone could be heard. And then he said, "The news? The news is that the sound is an A, it has always been an A and it always will be an A."

Each time my good friend refers to that tale I am reminded that it points up the importance of a "baseline," a consistent starting point from which all things began and are measured. The architect uses a straightedge or a T square, the chemist, certain weights and measures, the physicist employs an atomic clock, and the navigator, the stars. With each there is a guarantee of consistency and rightness of direction.

But how is one to measure history? What is the baseline for determining performance under stressful situations?

Where is the measurement for right and wrong?

The Christian, of course, might resort to several answers. Is not the supreme revelation of Jesus Christ, his words, his life-style, and his power an eternal baseline? Is not the Scripture itself a moral and spiritual measurement by which the actions and affections of people are to be measured? In both cases the answer is a certain yes.

But in every generation God also calls men and women to both live and speak in representation of his revelation. Such a person was Isaiah, the contemplative. As he communed with his God, there grew with him a confidence of opinion and judgment (some might also call it wisdom) that caused him to comment upon the turbulent events as they were happening around him. As the model contemplative he could not only perceive but he must also communicate that which he saw even if the message was unpopular.

If the tone of the tuning fork represents the rightness of a message and its spiritual baseline, I am also caused to think of the role of the concertmaster at the beginning of a concert. One hundred twenty musicians sit poised with their instruments ready to play, but before the conductor can come to the podium and begin the evening's selections of music the concertmaster must stand and sound a tone which he has received from the tuning fork or from the oboe. When the tone has been registered, all instruments are tuned to it. If one instrument is out of tune the music will be affected. The greatest orchestra in the world is useless in terms of producing the kind of music we expect to hear if each of its instrumentalists have not submitted to the sound of the tone that the concertmaster gives. And of course it goes without saying that if the concertmaster is unwilling to sound the tone that the tuning fork or the oboe has given to him, then the process is also sabotaged.

Isaiah's role as a commentator on public affairs is vividly portrayed in his encounter with Ahaz, king of Jerusalem.

Two kings to the north, Pekah (King of Israel) and Rezin (King of Syria) had formed a military alliance. Sensing that their common and dominant neighbor, Assyria, might be preoccupied enough by other international matters so as to be vulnerable to a sneak attack, Pekah and Rezin determined to put together a combined invasion force that would have a chance of military success. Obviously they felt that Ahaz's participation in the alliance was a necessity if their plan was to succeed, but Ahaz did not agree.

Approached by the kings of Israel and Syria, Ahaz continually refused, choosing to remain neutral. A glance at an ancient map will show that Ahaz was not an unwise strategist. After all, Assyria did not have a contiguous border with Judah and both Israel and Syria played the role of buffer states quite well. It was not within Ahaz's interest to join Pekah and Rezin. Furthermore, Jerusalem had generally plotted an independent and certainly neutral political course for several centuries and was decidedly inexperienced in the worlds of alliances and treaty organizations.

Pekah and Rezin, however, were not to be refused. Assuming that pressure might change Ahaz's mind, they sent their own armies southward through Judah until for a time they asserted control over almost all of the nation with the exception of the capital city of Jerusalem itself. Projections for Ahaz's future at that moment were not good. It was under such conditions that one reads of the mood of the city:

When the house of David [Ahaz] was told, "Syria is in league with Ephraim," his heart and the heart of his people shook as the trees of the forest shake before the wind. [Isa. 7:2]

Jerusalem must not have been a happy place to live during such moments. Obviously Ahaz did not have the character traits of leadership that his grandfather Uzziah had enjoyed for fifty years. Intelligence reports were frightening. Estimates of military strength massed against Jerusalem by the two combined northern armies created a mood of intimidation, and the morale of the entire city from the king to the poorest peasant can only be described as depressing. Opinion seemed unanimous. Jerusalem could not hold out under such circumstances.

But it wasn't unanimous after all. If it is true that the hearts of the people shook in fear like Ahaz, there was at least one important exception and that was Isaiah, who by now had learned to look at turbulent events from a different perspective. The same times, the same circumstances, the same possibilities—but a different perspective. Why? Isaiah's touch with his God is the only answer. Here is contemplative leadership and witness in motion in a commentary sort of way.

Isaiah wrote:

For the Lord spoke thus to me with his strong hand upon me, and warned me *not to walk in the way of this people*, saying: "Do not call conspiracy all that this people call conspiracy, and do not fear what they fear, nor be in dread. But the Lord of hosts, him you shall regard as holy; let him be your fear, and let him be your dread." [Isaiah 8:11-13, italics added]

Given that point of view and invested with God's "strong hand," Isaiah set out to comment upon events and point up different possibilities, options, and consequences.

Isaiah's encounter with Ahaz offers a magnificent insight into the role of the contemplative representative of God. It points up the dramatic contrast in people's appraisal of the same events when their baselines of perspective differ. We already know where Ahaz's thoughts are. He was terrified and depressed. Doubtless he has already contemplated a change of mind in his original refusal to Pekah and Rezin.

But one must always be careful when the majority agrees to the same course of action. Thus it was that Isaiah became extremely careful. What caused him to act differently? First, a direct message from God:

And the Lord said to Isaiah "Go forth to meet Ahaz . . . and say to him, "Take heed, be quiet, do not fear, and do not

let your heart be faint because of these two smoldering
stumps of firebrands, at the fierce anger of Rezin and
[Pekah] . . ."

In other words, if Ahaz would listen to the comments of
Isaiah he would really have no reason to fear events as he
saw them.

Then again, Isaiah was also operating from a second and
more general awareness. He knew that Jerusalem—as
God's holy city—had always enjoyed the covenant
promise that it would be unassailable as long as the kings of
every generation were faithful to God and his laws. It had
been God's message to David and God's long-term promise
to every king that followed him. Isaiah was simply
speaking out of the depth of that awareness. This was the
contemplative prophet giving a different commentary on
history than Ahaz was hearing from any other source.

I wonder how many contemporary Christians ever
ponder the same opportunity. Are there enough of those
men and women alive today whose sharpened spiritual
instincts give them confidence and authority to make
similar comments on the various sectors of life in the
world today?

Elton Trueblood wrote:

The Christian who wishes to be truly modern will have
to pay the price of rigorous thinking, for cheap modernity is
transparently ineffective and really deludes nobody. Does
anyone really believe that the gospel is better received if its
presentation is accompanied by the use of a guitar? If
contemporary prophets wish to make their maximum
contribution to the improvement of society, they should
try to deal not with organizational tricks, but with
exciting truth. [*New Man For Our Time* (New York:
Harper & Row, 1970)]

The English thinker, Harry Blamiers, writing in a book
entitled *The Christian Mind*, shows vast concern that
there are very few Christians about today who are
prepared to confront the Ahazes of our generation.

Prophetic condemnation of salient features of contemporary secularism come nowadays from secularists themselves whose ground of judgement is a humanistic one. It is clear that where there is no Christian mind to pass judgement upon society, those who are for human dignity and integrity on other grounds than the Christians will be provoked to rebel against multifarious tendencies of contemporary civilization to depersonalize men and women. This rebellion must be regarded as a significant feature of the post-Christian world. It is good in itself. That is to say, the protest needs to be made. *What is bad is that it should come from outside the Christian tradition.* [*The Christian Mind* (Ann Arbor, MI: Servant, 1978, paper)]

Blamiers simply decries the fact that there are very few with the commentary powers of an Isaiah who are prepared to speak as a tuning fork speaks about the eternal truths of God as applied to our contemporary generation and its antics.

The corporate executive, for example, needs the benefit of contemplative comment to sensitize him or her to moral and spiritual dimensions of business that others are not speaking about. So do the public servants; so do the law enforcement and military officer; so does the educator. But who is speaking? I grow increasingly alarmed over the absence of deep, perceptive, insightful comments on the great matters of debate which convulse our turbulent times while far too many Christians remain silent with either nothing to say or who seem too intimidated to say it. Blamiers seems to be sensing this when he writes:

Christianity is emasculated of its intellectual relevance. It remains a vehicle of spirituality and moral guidance at the individual level perhaps; at the communal level it is little more than an expression of sentimentalized togetherness.

In the decades which just closed, too few Christians had much to say about the great national debates on poverty, corruption, and war. Was it that God has no interest in these matters or simply that too few people are intimate with God in order to speak as Isaiah the contemplative was able to speak in his day.

If you boil down the role of the commentator to a simple action, it is to help the listener sort out choices and consequences. That is what Isaiah did for Ahaz. The choice for the king was a relatively simple one. He could trust in Isaiah's God, who promised that Jerusalem's enemies would fail, or the king would have to find some human answer to his dilemma.

It was quickly apparent that Ahaz was not going to listen to Isaiah. Even when offered an opportunity to choose a sign that would corroborate God's faithfulness his mind remained closed. He simply wasn't going to listen to Isaiah's comments and evaluations on the matter. As Isaiah listened to the refusal of Ahaz did his mind snap back to the day of the original vision in the temple when God had warned him that few, if any, would ever listen to his insights and his perspectives?

The writer of 2 Kings fills in the blanks of the story of Ahaz and his choices. Rather than face hostile force with God's promises and power, Ahaz chose to meet force with more force. A series of forces to be exact. A letter was drafted by Ahaz couched in the most flattering of terms and was sent to the Assyrian king, Tiglath-pileser: "I am your servant and your son. Come up, and rescue me from the hand of the king of Syria and from the hand of the king of Israel, who are attacking me" (2 Kings 16:7).

With the letter went gifts of silver and gold which were taken, ironically enough, from the temple where they had been part of the offerings given to God over the years in Jerusalem's acts of worship.

A quick analysis of Ahaz's pathetic letter to Tiglath-pileser points up the same theme one ordinarily associates with personal submission to God. And what compounds the tragedy is that the contents of this letter, minus the monetary gifts, would have sufficed to have gained the promised gracious intervention of God on Jerusalem's side in the first place.

It is a dramatic illustration of the difference between

the one who contemplatively learns to listen to and respond to the God of history and those who choose to live on the surface, putting their trust in numbers, firepower, intimidating personalities, and political options. It is not oversimplistic to suggest that it is also the fundamental issue which is determining the demise of Western civilization as we know it today.

Civilization's future is wrapped up in today's choices. One is reminded of a comment made recently by former Vice-President Walter Mondale who asked the question of the American public, "Are we wise enough to be smart?"

The simple fact of the matter is that Ahaz wasn't very wise and therefore he wasn't smart. Perhaps at first some people did credit Ahaz with having made a good decision. The letter and the gifts did indeed work, and before long Tiglath-pileser was moving southward from Assyria, neutralizing Syria and Israel with his armies. Ahaz was indeed spared; Jerusalem did not fall as everyone had thought it would. Events made it seem as if Ahaz had scored a diplomatic triumph.

But for every choice there is a corresponding consequence, and that is a spiritual principle as old as creation itself. What Isaiah had been concerned about in the beginning was to get Ahaz to see that the protection of Jerusalem was not the ultimate objective. Rather, the spiritual vitality of Jerusalem was far more important than its military safety. Ahaz had only been concerned about a primary and momentary objective of keeping the city impregnable. Isaiah had the long-range view and that accounts for the choices he urged Ahaz to make. Stanley Jones often warned his listeners that God always gives us the right of choice-making but not the right of consequence-choosing. Ahaz did indeed make a choice; and now the consequence was out of his control.

When the wars had ended, the Bible says that Ahaz traveled to Damascus to visit Tiglath-pileser. Call it a summit conference to express appreciation. While in Damascus the king of Jerusalem became enamored of an enormous statue used in the worship of pagan gods. A model of the idol was constructed and sent back to

Jerusalem. When Ahaz returned home, a full scale replica was virtually completed and before long it had been moved into the temple area to a position of prominence. The choice to trust pagan firepower rather than divine intervention had now come full circle. Jerusalem might be militarily free but it was already under spiritual assault. Now the worship of pagan gods was a daily routine in Jerusalem. The spiritual cancer caused by the choice and consequences of Ahaz became the seed of Jerusalem's eventual collapse and destruction many years later. Even though there were seeming moments of spiritual recovery and renewal, Jerusalem was never really the same, and it all started when Ahaz refused Isaiah's perspective on contemporary events.

When God told Isaiah to be cautious not to label as conspiracy that which the majority—including the king—said about affairs, he was effectively striking the heavenly tuning fork, reminding Isaiah to listen for and to sound the A. He was calling Isaiah to a larger view of history which placed all events within a heavenly context. Someone had to be there in the role of commentator to both inform the king and also to give him guidance should he choose to listen.

The turbulent eighties and nineties of this century have need of men and women similar to Isaiah, the commentator. History is capable today of being blasted back into some sort of medieval period because of the choices of people who are warped by greed and corruption. It is a time when Christians are correct in thinking that it is possible that the return of Christ may be just around the corner.

But there is also enough historical precedent to suggest that the return of Christ need not happen at this time. It is just as reasonable to pose the sobering thought that God may indeed permit the human race to stagger its way through the coming decades, continuing to play out its rebellious patterns of life as, in Paul's words, people further attempt to suppress the truth about God.

Many Christians have been adept at describing the conditions in which our Lord might just return for the entire world to see him. But too few have also summoned

insight and courage to face an alternative possibility.
There is need to face the times of historic turbulence with
the confidence of an Isaiah and give constant comment
to its elements. What indeed are the implications if we as
Christians and the church at large are to remain around in
history for a long time to come?

A reading of the book of Isaiah gives many examples of
the prophet in the role of the contemplative commentator.
He has much to teach us. For example, while others were
constantly impressed with the trappings of national power,
the prophet dismissed it all with a contemptuous wave of
both voice and pen:

The nations roar like the roaring oᶜ many waters, but [God]
will rebuke them, and they will flee far away, chased like
chaff on the mountains before the wind and whirling dust
before the storm. [Isa. 17:13]

Today nations are appraised by the size of their gross
national product, the availability of natural resources, their
will and ability to launch weapons, and the relative size
of their populations and accumulated wealth. But even
these sets of criteria are becoming increasingly suspect as
we watch small bands of dedicated terrorists paralyze major
governments, keeping them from bringing their might to
bear on new forms of enemy and opposition. A new sort of
fear arises as people become increasingly uncertain as to
who it is that has the real power to assert national will.

This is all that Isaiah is really saying. He is not
awestruck by the assembling of soldiers and military
hardware for a holiday parade. Neither is he overwhelmed, like others, when hostile forces make forays
deep into the homeland. As a contemplative, he sees into
things, not on their surface. He is sensitive to the spiritual
and moral dimensions of history, and therefore what
intimidates others—like a powerful nation state—tragically
amuses him.

When asked to assess national power, Isaiah seems only
to have had one concern. Is the nation's destiny
submitted to the God of all creation? If not, its days are

numbered. Whatever its racial and cultural configuration, its submission to God's authority is all important to Isaiah the commentator.

The German theologian, Dietrich Bonhoeffer, seems to have held this same view when he frequently commented on the affairs of the Third Reich during the 1930s. His biographers tell of a famous radio sermon on the German network the night Hitler was inducted into power. The text of Bonhoeffer's sermon? A commentary on the convictions and choices of Hitler's philosophy, a warning to the German people of the logical extension of these things. When all others were seeing things Hitler's way, Bonhoeffer was listening to a different tuning fork and he was perceptive enough to sense divergent and dangerous moments ahead. He was not swayed or lulled to sleep by the great promises of an invigorated economy and growing national pride.

Bonhoeffer never finished that sermon. Authorities cut him off the air. Fifteen years later he was dead, hanged by representatives of the same system he had warned about when it first came to power.

Isaiah was not afraid to come to similar conclusions about various types of personalities who possess leadership and notoriety in Jerusalem's social whirl. While most people fawned over kings wrapped in their splendid robes and symbols of position, Isaiah looked beyond the surface and appraised "haughty looks" and reminded whoever would listen that smirks of self-reliance "shall be brought low, and the pride of men shall be humbled; and the Lord alone will be exalted in that day" (Isa. 2:11).

While some lived only in the present, Isaiah added to his vision the long-range viewpoint. He warned leaders who flaunted their rebellious attitudes. "For the Lord of hosts has a day against all that is proud and lofty, against all that is lifted up" (Isa. 2:12).

Isaiah would have enjoyed the fairy tale, "The Emperor Who Had No Clothes." He refused to be impressed by beautiful uniforms. Rather, he saw the nakedness that was caused by inner cowardice. He knew that most of Jerusalem's powerful people had no courage, that they would run at the slightest provocation. Commenting upon them he said, "All your rulers have fled together, without the bow they were captured. All of you [the people of Jerusalem] who were found captured though they had fled away."

It was Isaiah's way of warning people that their leaders were not the sort who would stick around when the consequences of their choices became evident and the going got rough. One is tempted to compare Isaiah's viewpoint with pictures of the recent past when leadership has evacuated more than one falling city or embassy in helicopters while the populace who had trusted that same leadership was left to the mercy of the invading enemy.

When others took pride in an economic and political system that seemed to be working, Isaiah took another glance and said:

Your princes are rebels and companions of thieves. Everyone loves a bribe and runs after gifts. They do not defend the fatherless, and the widow's cause does not come to them. [Isaiah 1:23]

And he finally would warn the people, "your leaders mislead you and confuse the course of your paths."

One wonders what an Isaiah would have said on a number of occasions in our own recent history had he watched such things as shuttle diplomacy, the Paris peace talks, and the often incredible hypocrisy of international figures who meticulously draft documents carefully worded to please all ears but really end up saying nothing. The contemplative commentator watched diplomats of his own day attempt to iron out agreements and treaties, and he watched generals construct high walls and organize large armies in the hopes of insuring peace, and then he wrote: "Thou wilt keep him in perfect peace, whose mind is stayed on thee: because he trusteth in thee. Trust in the Lord forever for in the Lord Jehovah is everlasting strength" (Isa. 26:3, 4, KJV).

Again it was the striking of the heavenly tuning fork. Peace depended, Isaiah believed, on the moral and

spiritual fiber of Jerusalem. While others were content with
a negotiated peace that matched armies and hardware,
Isaiah saw the possibilities of a "perfect peace" that wasn't
purchased through a loss of integrity or sovereignty. A
peace that relied upon the promises of God was Isaiah's
prime objective.

A sense of frustration must have surged through Isaiah's
spirit when he stood before Ahaz and virtually begged
him to ask God for a confirming sign. So weak was Ahaz's
personal history of faith that God was more than willing
to come the extra distance to bolster his faith. But Ahaz
wouldn't even budge to that extent. He would get peace
in his own way he had decided.

When Isaiah commented upon the religious system of
the day, his pen seemed dipped in acid. While the
majority of the population saw the priests of the temple in
their intense piety, Isaiah saw and commented upon
something else.

The priest and the prophet reel with strong drink, they are
confused with wine, they stagger with strong drink; they
err in vision, they stumble in giving judgment. For all
tables are full of vomit, no place is without filthiness.
[Isa. 28:7, 8]

He stood on the sidelines and studied services and
ceremonies and refused to be impressed with high
attendance patterns and magnificently produced programs.

And the Lord said: "Because this people draw near with
their mouth and honor me with their lips, while their
hearts are far from me, and their fear of me is a
commandment of men learned by rote; therefore behold,
I will again do marvelous things with this people, wonderful
and marvelous; and the wisdom of their wise men shall
perish, and the discernment of their discerning men shall
be hid." [Isa. 29:13, 14]

Again the contemplative looks within actions and
people and then comments. His measurements are

certainly not the same as ours. We who often measure things by the number of people who respond with enthusiasm; we who are attracted to youth, beauty and vitality; we who are drawn by those who can spin clever words and make people laugh. Isaiah searched for content while too many of us are merely concerned with the excitement of an event. Isaiah was marginally interested in the words of one's mouth; he listened for the beat of one's heart and wherever Isaiah went in his day he did not like what his perceptions brought to him.

The more Isaiah looked at the spiritual realities of Jerusalem's religious life, the more impressed he became with the people's unwillingness to listen or to hunger for truth. Rather, he saw a tendency for men and women to wrap themselves in a form of paralyzing self-deceit. He called them

. . . a rebellious people, lying sons, sons who will not hear the instruction of the Lord; who say to the seers, "See not"; and to the prophets, "Prophesy not to us what is right; speak to us smooth things, prophesy illusions, leave the way, turn aside from the path, let us hear no more of the Holy One of Israel." [Isa. 30:9-11]

A cartoon pictures a court bailiff asking a perspective witness to swear, "Do you swear to tell the truth, the whole truth and nothing but the truth, even if the timing is wrong?" The amusing cartoon contains a grain of very sober truth. All too often people prefer truth only if the timing is right. But if the timing is wrong and if the truth breeds discomfort, dis-ease, or disconcerting reality, it is time for the truth to be suppressed. What Isaiah is uncovering in his day is an ancient form of modern coverup.

Again the old contemplative must have remembered, even more vividly than ever before, the text of God's vision as he became increasingly aware of people's unwillingness to face the truth. He was watching a city choose to go the extra mile into deceit. They were not only ignorant of truth, now they chose to ask their religious leadership not even to search for the truth. In fact, they were asking leaders to go into untruthful paths themselves. Tell us, they were saying, what is convenient for us to hear. Don't depress us; don't frighten us; don't make us uncomfortable.

Recently my wife Gail and I spent five days in the northern wilderness of Maine in a canoe paddling down parts of the beautiful Penobscot River. In preparation for that trip, I gathered maps and descriptive books that would help me chart out the trip. Looking backward I realize now how much I allowed my own anticipation, my excitement at getting underway, and a sort of personal optimism that I could handle anything to run away with my ability to face truth.

On the second day of our canoe trip, Gail and I ran into a series of what canoeists know to be ledges and cataracts which in turn forced us to spend more than a day and a half making fifteen separate portages with our heavy canoe and its "duffle," our equipment. On a few of those occasions we were actually in dangerous situations where either one of us could have been badly hurt or even killed. The ultimate result of the delay and the exhausting portages was that our trip had to end many, many miles short of our original goal. We came out of the water bruised and bug-bitten.

When we returned home, I got out the books describing the route we had taken. Sure enough, the warnings about the ledges and the waterfalls were there. Perhaps not as clearly as they ought to have been; but they were there. I had chosen to skim over those descriptions because I was confident in my enthusiasm and pride that they could be handled.

It was then that I began to recall to my secret horror that my neighbor, Ben, had said something about the danger of that particular part of the river. After all, he had fished that part of the river on many occasions. But I had dismissed his warnings because I have learned that Ben is always the cautious type anyway (he is forever inspecting his car, his lawn mower, his furnace). So I didn't listen to Ben. I really didn't want to hear truth, whether it came

from a book or from my neighbor who likes me enough
to warn me. And while I survived, our trip was cut
drastically short. One is reminded of the words of T. S.
Elliot who once wrote:

*Why should men love the church? Whey should they love
her laws?*
*She tells them of life and death, and of all they would
forget.*
*She is tender where they would be hard, and hard where
they would be tender.*
She tells them of evil and sin, and other unpleasant facts.

I can almost hear Isaiah listening to my account of the
aborted canoe trip and saying something about the fact
that I would have felt right at home among the religious
leadership of his day in Jerusalem if that is the way I run
the rest of my life. Those people didn't like truth either if it
threatened the status quo, or the well-being of people, or
if it dampened enthusiasm. And when someone came
forward with a comment based upon a heavenly baseline,
most of those people found creative ways to muzzle it all.
Who wants a commentator who makes people feel
uncomfortable?

The contemplative commentator knew that his nation
could not endure much more of the sort of dry rot that was
infesting the leadership of the day. Was Isaiah getting too
extreme when he wrote:

The whole head is sick, and the whole heart is faint. From
the sole of the foot even to the head, there is no soundness
in it, but bruises and sores and bleeding wounds; they are
not pressed out, or bound up, or softened with oil. [Isa.
1:5, 6]

In a premedical era Isaiah's allusion to festering sores is
prolific. The nation he loved was like a wound where the
poisonous pus was not pressed out. The wound had not
been bound so as to provide the possibilities of healing
and oil had not been poured upon all of it in order to keep it
clean, moist, and pliable. The national wound was not a
pretty sight, neither was the city.

Wherever Isaiah went he made comment upon the sickness of the city as he saw it. Beautiful women, he said,

are haughty and walk with outstretched necks, glancing wantonly with their eyes, mincing along as they go, tinkling with their feet; the Lord will smite them with a scab, the heads of the daughters of Zion, and the Lord will lay bare their secret parts.

He saw the eventual sorrow women would face when the men upon whom they depended were gone:

Your men shall fall by the sword and your mighty men in battle. And her gates shall lament and mourn; ravaged, she shall sit upon the ground. And seven women shall take hold of one man in that day, saying, "We will eat our own bread and wear our own clothes, only let us be called by your name; take away our reproach." [Isa. 3:25—4:1]

It was Isaiah's way of saying to women, you can act the way you choose today because your security seems to be guaranteed, but there is coming a turbulent day when your security will be absent. How will you act then?

Probably nothing caused Isaiah to swing into prophetic commentary more than his sense of their personal pride. Commenting on the pride of Jerusalem when the people thought themselves to be part of an impregnable fortress, he wrote:

Woe to those who hide deep from the Lord their counsel, whose deeds are in the dark, and who say, "Who sees us? Who knows us?" You turn things upside down! Shall the potter be regarded as the clay; that the thing should say of its maker, "He did not make me"; or the thing formed say of him who formed it, "He has no understanding"? [Isa. 29:15, 16]

This is the Jerusalem over which Isaiah, the contemplative commentator spiritually presided. He took no joy in the direction that they were going. He felt no personal satisfaction that his predictions were coming true. Rather, there was ache in his heart as he saw the destiny of kings and people and where their unending series of destructive choices were taking them.

The role of the contemplative is not an easy or a happy one. In a sense, the contemplative can never be a happy person most of the time. He or she knows far too much. Only satisfaction remains in keeping intimate with the promises and assurances of the eternal God.

There have been many, over the centuries, who have attempted to write much in the same vein of an Isaiah, having seen the same things about their own generation. Elton Trueblood wrote soon after the end of World War II about American society

The terrible danger of our time consists in the fact that ours is a cut flower civilization. Beautiful as cut flowers may be, and much as we use our ingenuity to keep them looking fresh for awhile, they will eventually die. And they die because they are severed from their sustaining roots

Elton Trueblood continues his analysis of the day in which he lives by writing:

We are trying to maintain the dignity of the individual apart from the deep faith that every man is made in God's image and is therefore precious in God's eyes.
[*Predicament of Modern Man* (New York: Harper and Row, 1944)]

I think I hear Elton Trueblood warning us years ago that the same forces are in motion today as were in the day when Isaiah walked the streets of Jerusalem and saw things and commented upon them unlike anyone else of his time.

The music professor strikes the tuning fork and the instruments are tuned. A new day of playing and evaluating music is begun with the same standard as has been followed on every other day when the fork struck. So it was with Isaiah. The contemplative began every day listening to the voice of God and what he heard caused him to make judgments and evaluations on the turbulent events of his generation. He didn't do it out of pride but out of the humility that first came to him when he saw himself in the temple. And out of that entire experience came comment, the kind that all of us desperately need today.

AXIOM FOURTEEN
A person for turbulent times does not stand in silence when the greedy, the rebellious, or the proud set forth in the pursuit of evil designs but is prepared to unleash holy anger towards those who deny the rightful blessings of creation to the poor and the helpless.

16/ Isaiah, the confronter

In his lectures, Malcolm Muggeridge has often been fond of quoting the words of the English poet, William Blake:

*This life's dim windows of the soul
Distort the heavens from pole to pole
And lead you to believe a lie
When you see with, not through, the eye.*

If Muggeridge has attempted to bring one message home to Western civilization in these latter Christian years of his life, it is this: seeing *with* one's eye invites destruction; seeing *through* the eye may enhance spiritual discrimination. Muggeridge is admittedly frightened. He senses the former alternative prevails in our day, while the latter continues to diminish.

The English humorist and author makes a serious point and one that may help us to appreciate another role of the contemplative Christian in each generation. For

Muggeridge is warning us that too many people find it
easy to "go with the flow," watching events rather than
interpreting them and assigning moral and spiritual
value to them.

To see *with* the eye is merely to be a spectator but to see
through the eye is to look into the center of things and
investigate meaning and purpose, to sort out choice and
consequence, to sense those issues which are according to
the purposes of God, the Creator, and those which are not.
Such an exercise may be a lonely one. It demands inner
discipline and constant communion with the living God.

When Isaiah walked the streets of Jerusalem, he gazed at
events and people *through* his eye. The visual data his eye
collected was mixed with the things his ears heard. All of
this was impressed upon his inner spirit, which
compared and contrasted it to the standards he knew to be
God's laws and ultimate purposes. No wonder there was
an enormous gulf between the conclusions to which Isaiah
the contemplative came and those of the majority who
walked the streets of that great city. Men and women like
him were frequently in trouble with those who cared
little about eternal or heavenly standards. More than
once they were denounced by the opinion-makers in no
uncertain terms.

On one occasion, for example, a generation or two
before Isaiah's time when the kings of Judah and Israel had
been on better terms, there had been conversation about
the wisdom of combining national armies and going to war
against a common enemy. Because it was the acceptable
thing to do, a part of the kings' advance planning had been
to consult the so-called prophets of their day, men so
phony and false that they were nothing more than religious
fortune-tellers.

Apparently the "prophets" were unanimous in telling
the kings what they wanted to hear; they all predicted
victory. But the king of Judah remained strangely unsettled
over these reports and asked, "Is there not here another
prophet of the Lord of whom we may inquire?"

A reading of the text in 2 Chronicles causes me to
imagine the tension in the moment as Ahab, the king of

Israel, pondered the question. Inwardly, Ahab must have groaned and writhed as he agonized over what to say and for some reason he felt compelled to come clean. Thus he said, "There is yet one man by whom we may inquire of the Lord, Micaiah . . . but I hate him for he never prophesies good concerning me, but always evil" (2 Chron. 18:7).

Similar examples abound of the trouble that arose when faithful men who saw events *through* the eye spoke the truth. Jeremiah was slandered, called unpatriotic. Ezekiel was cheered for his eloquence but ignored when it came to obeying the content of his preaching. Others were exiled, imprisoned, and even killed. No wonder the temptation becomes overwhelming for many people to turn off the facilities of the inner spirit. The judgments generated from one who is in touch with God are often too much in contrast with the prevailing opinions of those who appear to be in momentary control of events.

But it is not enough to simply have opinions, negative or positive. As we have already learned in the life of Isaiah, to be endowed with the sort of insight that Isaiah possessed was to speak boldly and frankly. And there were times when that meant that the contemplative prophet played the role not only of commentator, who helped others sort out choices, but that he must also be confronter, who pointed out the certainty of consequences.

Confrontation means forcing people to face truth about themselves and their choices. It is a major biblical theme. Young pastors were challenged by their mentors in the days of the Early Church to rebuke those who were soft on sin. The writer of Hebrews pressed his readers to "exhort one another every day as long as it is called 'today,' that none of you may be hardened by the deceitfulness of sin" (Heb. 3:13). Paul confronted the Corinthians on a broad range of matters, from theological heresy to relational breakdown, from sexual impropriety to materialistic greed. In each case the effort was aimed at helping people see that certain of their choices were taking them head-on into consequences that were plainly spiritually and morally destructive.

Isaiah exhausted himself in constant confrontation with

Jerusalem's leaders and their prevailing thought. For example, he watched each successive king in his own lifetime formulate a national defense policy based on military might rather than on spiritual depth. Isaiah's formula for peace and security was simple: "in returning [repentance] and rest [worship] you shall be saved; in quietness and trust shall be your strength."

But Isaiah's spiritual policy went unheeded. Weapons of warfare seemed far more the logical response to mounting enemy pressure which seemed to be coming from all sides. Thus, Isaiah warned: "you said 'No! We will speed upon horses,' therefore you shall speed away; and, 'We will ride upon swift steeds,' therefore your pursuers will be swift." His analysis was simple. It would make no difference how large and well equipped Jerusalem's armies were. The enemy would always be larger in number and more powerful in weaponry.

In such clashes of policy the contemplative prophet and the frightened kings of Jerusalem grew further and further apart in the way they saw things. The former looked *through* his eyes from the depths of a spirit communing with God; the latter looked *with* the eyes and relied on human strategy and intellect.

Throughout his prophetic vocation Isaiah was relentless in confronting people with the implications of their choices. When the king of Jerusalem sent diplomats southward to Egypt to form an alliance that would provide military weaponry and backup manpower, Isaiah said:

"Woe to the rebellious children," says the Lord, "who carry out a plan, but not mine; and who make a league, but not of my spirit, that they may add sin to sin; who set out to go down to Egypt, without asking for my counsel, to take refuge in the protection of Pharaoh, and to seek shelter in the shadow of Egypt!" [Isa. 30:1, 2]

Later Isaiah would warn: "Egypt's help is worthless and empty." Not reluctant to mix his comments with sarcasm, he went on, "therefore I have called her 'Rahab who sits still.' " (Isa. 30:7)

Is Isaiah the only person of his generation who has a sense of history? Why, he seemed to be wondering, would the people of God go back to Egypt and ask for help from a society that had long ago sucked them dry of their energies and spirit when they had enslavement? Again, here was the contemplative spirit in motion. It remembered the lessons of history and projected them into the possible consequences of the future.

Nowhere is confrontation more aptly illustrated than in Isaiah's relationship to Hezekiah, the fourth king of Jerusalem during the prophet's lifetime. Two separate incidents, years apart, served to illustrate ways in which confrontation can happen.

The first of the two experiences occurred when the Assyrian army under the generalship of its king, Sennacherib, marched southward on a campaign that threatened to inundate the entire Middle East. The buffer states of Syria and Israel were now non-existent; nothing stood in the way of Sennacherib's forces as they marched toward Jerusalem.

Looking around the city and camping south of it at Lachish, Sennacherib sent negotiators to Jerusalem's city walls. Hezekiah was powerless and he knew it. His message to Sennacherib? "I have done wrong; withdraw from me; whatever you impose on me I will bear." The Assyrian was only too glad to send back a bill, and thus it was that:

Hezekiah gave him all the silver that was found in the house of the Lord, and in the treasuries of the king's house. At that time Hezekiah stripped the gold from the doors of the temple of the Lord, and from the doorposts which Hezekiah king of Judah had overlaid and gave it to the king of Assyria. [2 Kings 18:15 ff.]

One wonders what Isaiah must have thought as he watched from the shadows this sad dismantling of the temple's beauty and wealth to feed Sennacherib's greed.

What price was being paid because one more king of Jerusalem resisted trusting in the promise God had made to David years before that the city would not fall as long as its people were faithful!

But even then Hezekiah's humiliation was not ended. Sennacherib and his men were less than honorable because, in spite of Hezekiah's tribute, they returned with a follow-up demand that the city surrender. Another conference was scheduled. Enemy negotiators offered this proclamation:

On what do you rest this confidence of yours? Do you think that mere words are strategy and power for war? On whom do you now rely, that you have rebelled against me? Behold, you are relying now on Egypt, that broken reed of a staff which will pierce the hand of any man who leans on it. Such is Pharaoh, king of Egypt to all who rely on him.

As if to further intimidate Hezekiah and the city, Sennacherib's people added insult to injury:

Come now, make a wager with my master the King of Assyria; we will give you two thousand horses, if you are able on your part to set riders upon them. How can you repulse a single captain among the least of my master's servants, when you rely on Egypt for chariots and for horsemen?

There must have been a host of smirks as Sennacherib's men toyed with those of Hezekiah. There was no contest, and everyone knew it. It was as Isaiah had earlier commented: rely on your army and the enemy will have a better one.

If anyone needed any further evidence of Hezekiah's helplessness in this situation, it is found in the futile response of the negotiators sent out from Jerusalem just beyond the walls to respond to Sennacherib's lieutenants:

Pray, speak to your servants in the Aramaic language, for we understand it; do not speak to us in the language of Judah within the hearing of the people on the wall.

Censorship, that's what it was. The situation was so bad
that Hezekiah's staff quickly realized that if the people
on the walls knew the full extent of the truth about
Hezekiah's untenable position, they might be tempted to
take the situation into their own hands and surrender the
city out of fear.

Sennacherib's men knew that too, and rather than agree to
the request, they simply stepped out in front of the walls
where the people listened and addressed the populace
directly, repeating the realities of the situation . . . this
time in even greater detail. Hezekiah's only response was to
order the people not to reply.

It was only under such turbulent conditions that
Hezekiah finally turned to Isaiah. Having ignored
Isaiah's original platform for a heaven-guaranteed peace,
having given away the temple and national treasure, and
now having faced total humiliation, he was ready to
consult with God's contemplative man on the spot.

As a pastor, I am all too familiar with the ethos of such a
moment: A proud man or woman who has for years
coasted on the surface successes of business ventures,
physical health or beauty, and a lot of "good luck." Then
a crash of sorts occurs: a marriage which cracks under
increasing strain, a child who grows rebellious and
unreachable, a once solid career turns sour. There are a host
of variations on this tragic theme. I get no satisfaction
from such moments but as I grow older I see how predictable
they are. "Be not deceived," Paul wrote, "God is not
mocked. What a man sows, he reaps. . . ."

In this case, Hezekiah was reaping what he and others
before him had been sowing for years. They had had no
business playing the game of international power politics.
Others might, but this was not to have been the lot of a city
like Jerusalem, whose political and social foundations were
founded on the supernatural guidance and protection of
Jehovah. One does not preserve what God has given through
ungodly methods and means. And when choices are made to
do just that, then it is predictable that God will allow the
consequences to take their course.

It is in those kinds of circumstances that the advisors of
Hezekiah went to Isaiah saying,

This day is a day of distress, of rebuke, and of disgrace; children have come to birth, and there is no strength to bring them forth. It may be that the Lord your God heard all the words of [Sennacherib's emissary], whom his master, the king of Assyria has sent to mock the living God, and will rebuke the words that the Lord your God has heard; therefore lift up your prayer for the remnant that is left.

Only a man of tremendous self-respect would have avoided a moment of gloating, private self-satisfaction at this stunning admission of impotence. Perhaps, in contrast, there is a reechoing of the question he had once asked God in that special vision: "Lord, how long does this sort of thing have to go on?"

There are in the words of Hezekiah's message to Isaiah the seeds of repentance. He seems to be saying that he had seen how incredibly stupid he had been. Is deliverance possible at this late hour?

It is a commentary on God's grace that even now in this final hour of seeming defeat, he was not impervious to the desperate cry for help. Really, it is as close to a deathbed conversion as one might dare to get. But out of this candid admission that there was no other hope, a flicker of spiritual remission became possible. In turning to Isaiah's unorthodox policy of depending upon God for Jerusalem's salvation, there may be deliverance.

This was Isaiah the contemplative confronter, facing the consequences of bad choices and bringing a fresh word from God that included deliverance and restoration. Again he was just the person for turbulent times. Compare this moment with the one Joseph had shared with Pharaoh centuries before when all human resources seemed also to have failed. On both occasions, one man with a hand on heaven stood between total confusion and sensible conclusion.

This example of confrontation ended in good news. Confrontation can happen only when the two parties involved are willing to face the facts as they are. Isaiah had been willing for some time to do that. But now it was

Hezekiah who was also ready to see things *through* the eye.
In the moment of defeat and powerlessness Hezekiah was
prepared to see things as God sees them. Thankfully the
contemplative was there to offer help and hope. Isaiah's
words:

Thus says the Lord: Do not be afraid because of the words
that you have heard, with which the servants of the king
of Assyria have reviled me. Behold, I will put a spirit in him,
so that he shall hear a rumor and return to his own land; and
I will cause him to fall by the sword in his own hand. [2
Kings 19:5]

And so it happened exactly as Isaiah predicted and
promised. Before further negotiations over the surrender of
Jerusalem could take place, word reached Sennacherib
back in Lachish that the Egyptians and Ethiopians were
headed in his direction and he averted his attention from
Hezekiah. He sent a short note to Hezekiah telling him
that he would get back to him as soon as he had dealt
with the Ethiopians. But Sennacherib never had a chance to
face Hezekiah again or even to return to his original demand
because an angel of the Lord, Scripture says, entered his
camp one night soon after and slew 185,000 soldiers.
Stripped of a substantial part of his military machine,
Sennacherib returned to Assyria to regroup and within a
few months was murdered by his two sons in an attempted
coup.
   An analysis of Isaiah's performance in this episode offers
several important insights about the role of a confronter
in turbulent times. Having stated his positions on the
issues of peace and security, Isaiah had stood back and let
matters take their course. His judgment told him that
Hezekiah would have to see the whites of the enemies'
eyes before he was prepared to change his mind and thus
Isaiah waited. And the waiting must have been
agonizing.
   Part of the genius of spiritual leadership is an
understanding of when people must be released to
experience the consequences of their choices no matter

what they may be. Once the issues have been clearly
described, the spiritual leader must often become silent.
Sometimes the youthful or the unwise spiritual leader
will try to live life for his or her people, never giving them
the chance to see and discover for themselves what only
they can learn. As it must have been with Isaiah, the waiting
for such moments is often agonizing.

But when the right time came, Isaiah was ready to
perform again and to offer words of grace. The
contemplative is perceptive enough to know when grace
is needed, when he or she is to bring words of forgiveness
and restoration. That was Isaiah's role at this time.

But the confronter had another role which seemed the
more harsh and painful. Years later Isaiah and Hezekiah
were to encounter one another again. While circumstances
were somewhat different, the themes were almost
identical.

Following the deliverance of the city, Hezekiah had set
out to restore the city's fortune. Wealth poured back into
the temple and into the national treasury. The city's
fortifications were rebuilt and strenghtened. A water supply
was tunneled into the center of the city from outside the
walls. Water had been one of Jerusalem's serious points of
vulnerability.

One gets the impression as he reads of Hezekiah's frantic
efforts to rebuild the city and its strength that the lesson
learned in the times of Sennacherib had been partially
forgotten. Hezekiah was a bit more faithful to the God of
Jerusalem to be sure but one wonders if he didn't also think
it wise to backstop faith just a bit and keep stockpiling
weapons and manpower, just in case.

The writer of the Chronicles describes Hezekiah's
recovery from the days of Sennacherib's humiliation:

Hezekiah had very great riches and honor; and he made for
himself treasuries for silver, for gold, for precious stones,
for spices, for shields, and for all kinds of costly vessels. . . .
He likewise provided cities for himself, and flocks and
herds in abundance; for God had given him very great
possessions. This same Hezekiah closed the upper outlet

of the waters of Gihon and directed them down the west side of the city of David. And Hezekiah prospered in all his works. [2 Chron. 32:27-30]

This description of events suggests that restoration in the life of a repentant king can be quite dramatic and successful. Isaiah must have watched this miraculous economic and military recovery and wondered at times where all of this was going to end. Indications are that once again the contemplative was being shoved to the background, not needed when things were going well. It is not a new observation to say that contemplatives and genuine prophets are not always welcome in times of prosperity and seeming security.

And so it was—in a time like that—that a second crisis arose over a period of a few years that would bring back Isaiah the contemplative to a front and center position on the stage of Jerusalem's life and into the experience once more of Hezekiah. But this time the confronter's work was of a different sort: necessarily more harsh and painful.

The Assyrian threat to national security was now relaxed. Babylon, the distant young upstart of a nation, was only beginning to show signs of its future imperialistic intent. And Jerusalem was enjoying its prosperity when Hezekiah suddenly became ill. The sickness was serious, and soon the king was preparing for the very worst. His impressions were confirmed when Isaiah entered his bedchamber one day and told him, "Thus says the Lord: set your house in order; for you shall die; you shall not recover."

Once again Hezekiah faced what appeared to be a no-win situation. Events were beyond his control. Fortified walls, water supplies, and immense amounts of silver, gold, and spices could not purchase life. Again and again under such circumstances the king was driven to look heavenward:

Then Hezekiah turned his face to the wall, and prayed to the Lord, saying, "Remember now, O Lord, I beseech thee, how I have walked before thee in faithfulness and with a

whole heart, and have done what is good in thy sight."
And Hezekiah wept bitterly. [2 Kings 20:2, 3]

As usual Hezekiah's prayer reached God, and Isaiah was
soon sent back to Hezekiah's bedside with the further
message that a period of fifteen years was being added to the
king's life. Isaiah, chapter 39, records the delirious
rejoicing that followed this pronouncement. Worship and
thanksgiving were the order of the day: "The Lord will
save me, and we will sing to stringed instruments all the
days of our life, at the house of the Lord."

But an analysis of Scripture suggests that his praise
hymn was soon forgotten. The clouds of an ultimate
crisis began to gather. A healed and invigorated Hezekiah
headed back to his throne of national leadership. His
reputation steadily grew, and before long word reached the
ears of the Babylonian leader that Hezekiah might be
worth meeting. Why? Because he was a potential obstacle to
their expansionistic plans for the future? Or because he
might be a potential ally (at least in the beginning) in a
Babylonian attempt to neutralize and then destroy
Assyria?

Whatever the reason, envoys arrived one day in the city
of Jerusalem bringing the greetings of Merodach-baladan,
king of Babylon, and extending best wishes and
congratulations concerning the complete recovery of
Hezekiah's health. Read between the lines, and you get
the feeling that Hezekiah was only too glad to receive these
visitors. He was flattered by their compliments and amused
by the attention being given the throne of Jerusalem.
When one is relatively small, it is nice to be given the big
league treatment by the major powers.

How does one act under such circumstances? That is the
big question that led to Hezekiah's final confrontative
encounter with Isaiah. Looking backward, there is no
doubt that Hezekiah's choices in this matter would go a
long way toward determining the future, not only for his life
and family but also for the entire city. The seduction of
men's applause is one of the greatest battles that any man
or woman of God will ever face. It is among the most

supreme tests that anyone in Christian leadership faces
today and so it was also in the life of Hezekiah.

And so in the matter of the envoys of the princes of
Babylon, who had been sent to him to inquire about the sign
that had been done in the land, God left Hezekiah to
himself, in order to try him and to know all that was in his
heart. [2 Chron. 32:31]

Isaiah, the *commentator* is not to perform here.
Hezekiah has had enough time to learn the ropes of
responsible decision-making. Past performance and
experience should have been quite adequate for him to
remember where lay the glory and the credit for
Jerusalem's fortune and his own health. Hezekiah was not
to be nursed along; he was not to be given all the answers
ahead of time. Here was the moment to find out if he had
learned to look beyond himself for appropriate wisdom
and judgment. Here was the time to look *through* and not
with the eye to see what the real issues were when the
Babylonians arrived.

And Hezekiah welcomed them; and he showed them his
treasure house, the silver, the gold, the spices, the
precious oil, his whole armory, all that was found in his
storehouses. There was nothing in his house or in all his
realm that Hezekiah did not show them. [Isa. 39:2]

Incredible! A man, only a short period of time before
weeping bitterly on his bed, face to the wall, desperate
just to keep on breathing and when visitors came inquiring
ostensibly about his recovered health, he set out to
impress upon them his own personal achievements in the
accumulation of wealth and power.
I am impressed with the amazing consistency of most
human performances over the years. The shape and value
of things held precious may have changed over the centuries,
but men and women still try just as hard to accrue glory
and power to themselves whenever possible—whenever
there is someone ready to ask questions and give cheap

applause. How easy it is to forget the God of salvation and restoration when prosperity seems to be ours. Perhaps it is a mystery as to why God permits anyone to become prosperous for so long. We seem to be so adept at mishandling it.

Christian leaders can be among the most vulnerable in this matter. Their wealth may not always be counted in terms of money or possessions but it is common to see a person highly gifted and effective drift into a pseudo-spirituality which increasingly delights in applause, connections, and privileges. All too often we see superstars of the religious world doting more upon their own charisma than the God who first entrusted it to them. It is, therefore, with great thankfulness that I look to certain men and women who have never let the adulation of the crowd deny them their integrity, the power of their message, and their simple, humble touch with the God of Jesus Christ. Not so with Hezekiah!

It was in the wake of this enormously successful visit from the Babylonian delegation that Isaiah once again entered the house of Hezekiah. This time his visit was not marked with good news. This time Isaiah was not there with words of deliverance and peace. This was the contemplative who looked at events through the eye from a heart in touch with God, and his duty at this time was to ask hard questions and confirm grim consequences. This was high-powered confrontation.

Watch the confronter in action this time, armed with a question:

Isaiah: "What did these men say? And whence did they come to you?"

Hezekiah: "They have come to me from a far country, from Babylon."

Isaiah: *"What have they seen in your house?"*

Hezekiah: "They have seen all that is in my house; there is nothing in my storehouses I did not show them."

That is all we know about the conversation between the two men and it is enough. The key was the question: "What have they seen in your house?" It forced the issue into the open; it brought Hezekiah to a point of painful awareness about his choice.

The Bible is replete with a series of embarrassing questions all asked in similar moments of confrontation. Jesus to Judas in the garden: "Friend, why are you here?" God to Cain: "Why are you angry? . . . where is your brother?" Paul to the Galatian congregation: "Who has bewitched you?" In each case the question is a form of confrontation. It has forced the listener to stop seeing *with* the eye and start seeing *through* it. The question is designed to bring the person to a point of personal realization, but how great has been the offense of their performance to date.

"What have they seen in your house?" How did you explain your greatness, Hezekiah? Where did you assign the credit for all this? What did those men return to Babylon thinking about you, about your God? The unasked question was this: "Hezekiah, what do the Babylonians know about the God who healed you? Made you prosperous? Saved your city in the first place? Nothing, right? They saw everything in your house—but God."

Later on, looking back on this encounter, Isaiah would say of Hezekiah:

In that day you looked to the weapons of the House of the Forest, and you saw that the breaches of the city of David were many, and you collected the waters of the lower pool, and you counted the houses of Jerusalem, and you broke down the houses to fortify the wall. You made a reservoir between the two walls for the water of the old pool. But you did not look to him who did it, or have regard for him who planned it long ago. [Isa. 22:8-11]

The original question (What have they seen?) and this simple statement were examples of Isaiah, the contemplative, who found it necessary to confront a man with the truth of his own deceit and willful ignorance of God's acts in his life. Someone had to blow the whistle, and it was Isaiah's responsibility to do the job.

Hear the word of the Lord of hosts: Behold, the days are coming, when all that is in your house, and that which your fathers have stored up till this day, shall be carried to Babylon; nothing shall be left, says the Lord. And some of your own sons, who are born to you, shall be taken away; and they shall be eunuchs in the palace of the king of Babylon. [Isa. 39:5-7]

Devastating judgment! How ironic that many of the things that Hezekiah proudly showed the Babylonian envoys would one day make their way into the coffers of the Babylonian kings. One wonders what is being revealed in the character of Hezekiah when it is recorded that his reaction was somewhat vitiated by the fact that the events of the judgment would happen only after he himself was dead and gone. "At least," he thought, "there will be peace and security in my days."

If there is an ugly side to the ministry in servanthood, it is in the area of confrontation. The contemplative, seeing events *through* the eye from a spirit charged with the presence of God, cannot escape the responsibility to speak about what he or she is seeing. But all too often, those who would claim a special presence from God are indeed silent. Silence perhaps from fear or silence because personal interests might also be threatened. It is a painful matter every time I have to raise an issue as a pastor that confronts people I find easy to love in my congregation, or those whose generosity or prominence seem indispensable to the church's future.

It is said that when Bonhoeffer looked upon the horrors of war as his own German nation was practicing it, he prayed for the defeat of his own people so that the world might know for a thousand years that the God of justice and righteousness looks harshly upon those who would make war.

There have been many turbulent times in our own land,

both on a national and local level, when it was time for those claiming a Christian orientation to speak out in confrontation against those whose actions were unjust, corrupt, and destructive. In the absence of such confrontation, men and women—both Christian and non-Christian—are all too often permitted to move in paths that lead to their own demise as well as those about them. This happens in companies, institutions, and even nations.

I am thankful that there were those with courage to ask hard questions about American involvement in Vietnam. What if no one had asked questions which led to the exposure of Watergate? Today there are new questions looming on the horizon which are indeed Christian in nature since they center on the well-being of people.

What of refugees around the world and our treatment of them, millions of them starving, without homes and basic human rights? Tens of thousands of people appear to be unjustly detained in prisons where they face beatings and torture. Companies have poured toxic chemicals into the earth's water supply and evidence increasingly arises that people now live with cancer, deformities, and early death because of it. An ethic which can only be called immoral has virtually wrested total control of the world of television, and our children's minds are regularly polluted with a worldview that is anti-God. An acceptance of abortion on demand seems to be cheapening our view of the preciousness of life. Selfishness pervades the feelings of many workers causing a decline in national productivity, and thus, many think, increasing the spiral of inflation. And beyond it all, a me-first attitude best illustrated in the title of Robert Ringer's best seller, *Looking Out for Number One* seems to have swept Western civilization.

Where are the contemplative confronters who will face these spiritual issues and many more like them that I have left unmentioned? This is an important part of the contemplative's role in the world: to confront with questions, embarrassing questions. He or she is the person seeing *through* the eye that is wired to the inner spirit, that says, "What have they seen in your house?"

Unless there are such people—like Isaiah—in motion, our civilization has little left for tomorrow. But confrontation also must take place on the individual level of the pursuit of our spiritual disciplines. Not only must we be willing to confront, we must be "confrontable." As I grow older I see more clearly that one of the great reasons that some men and women are spiritually prosperous and others are not is based upon their willingness to accept the confrontation of their spiritual mentors and even the comments of their enemies. Wisdom is desperately needed to see the difference between cheap and earned success. Judgment is desperately necessary if we are to understand the difference between eternal perspectives and temporal objectives. Confrontation helps us to sort out motives and moods, the quality of various methods and means.

Sometimes we need to even face the importance of self-confrontation. This can come as we study in a disciplined fashion the Word of God and let it speak to our own inner spirit. The writer of Hebrews warns us that the Word of God is sharp like a two-edged sword and can pierce to the very deepest parts and expose those inner thoughts that are actually within us. Dry and superficial the man or woman who never lays his life open to the straight-edged measurement of the Holy Scriptures. There must be times for brooding, for meditating in which the deepest thoughts can be analyzed and assessed. Sometime ago I wrote the following piece of bad poetry entitled, "Midnight Games." It tells the stories of two men, one of whom badly needed confrontation and somehow never got it. The consequences of their choices are vivid and not altogether unrealistic.

Midnight Games

Last night at a late hour
two men, unknown to each other,
sat brooding over fifty-five years of life.
There are those moments
when the proper ingredients of mood,

time, silence, fatigue, accomplishment
  or failure—
cause minds to gaze
across the sweep of existence,
playing a strange and ruthless game called
"What's it all about?"
Such ingredients being at that critical stage,
my two acquaintances
begin play.

One man sat at his desk
amongst paneled royalty
in his private den
surrounded by quadraphonic noise.
In such opulence, he thought.

The other rested callous hands
on a scratched kitchen table.
No sound afoot except
for the deep breathing of sleeping children
in the next room
and a humming wife,
preparing for bed.

"Tally the card,"
that part of man's being
which searches for accomplishment
said.
"Count the score," it cried; "make a report
you two men,
separated by railroad tracks,
square footage, horsepower, and clout."
And so the first of the two began.

For openers, I own a home, he said,
with three garages, each filled with imported cars
(I might as well say it).
The spread is lavish
  nothing spared to make it the best
  all around.
I own it all; it's paid for.
You could say that it's an estate.

I own a business, and
I own three hundred persons who work for me
  (I might as well own them).
  I tell them when they must come to work;
  I tell them when to eat,
  how much they'll earn,
  how hard they'll strive.
They call me "Mr."; some call me "Sir."
Yes, you could say that I own them.

I own a wife
(I might as well say it).
I've capped her teeth,
  imported Paris' finest,
  paid for weight reduction,
  dance lessons, club memberships.
I've purchased her cosmetic beauty.
Yes, you could say that I own her.

I own my kids
(I might as well say it).
I've paid off Harvard,
  Chevrolet, the optometrist,
  the abortionist.
I've set them in motion
  with trust funds,
  European vacations
  and front page weddings.
Yes, you could say that I own them.

I own my investments:
  my property, my stocks,
  my directorships
(I might as well say it).
I own my broker too.
Without me he'd go
  from broker to broke.
Yes, you could say that I've got
  everything I own under control.

I own a reputation;
some say hardnosed, others shrewd

(I might as well say it).
I am respected, if not loved.
   But I never started out to be loved;
   rather that men might tremble
   at my word and decision.
I have my reputation;
Yes, you could say that.

I guess I own just about everything.
Why then am I so empty of spirit
   as I play this midnight game?
Why do I sit here
   wondering:
      why my wife is not here,
      why my children chose other things to do,
      if my company will survive,
      if my reputation is secure,
      if anyone likes me.
Why must I wonder
   when I own it all?

Second half of match;
please leave that impressive scene;
cross the tracks,
count the score,
tally the card
of a second man
who plays the game.

My house is old; my car rusting out,
   and I wonder, he thinks,
   if the furnace will last the winter.
But (I might as well admit it)
this place owns me.
   It calls me to itself each evening
   As I walk three blocks
   from the bus stop.
It beckons with memories
   of Christmases, crisis,
   giggles and prayers.
I am gladly owned by its warmth.

My job . . . is a job, humbling;
   its income modest
But (I might as well admit it)
it kind of owns me—
   its opportunities to serve others,
   to fix things,
      make them go and click,
   to make something
      with these hands of mine,
   some sense of accomplishment
   producing finished things from raw.
You could say I like what I'm doing.

My wife, listen to her hum off key,
   was not a cheer leader,
   and Wellesley is not her background.
But (I might as well admit it)
   she owns me; I belong to her;
      so compelling her affection;
      so deep her insight;
      so broad her perspective;
      so eternal her values;
      so compassionate her caring.
I gladly give myself to her.
You could say that I am possessed,
   nothing held back.

My children; hear them toss in troubled sleep,
   average students,
   reasonable competitors.
They (I might as well be frank about it)
   own me.
I cannot withhold my time from them,
   my unrestrained enjoyment as
   they discover life and allow me
   to join them as both
   player and spectator.
The birth certificates say they are mine.
   But my heart says they own me.

As to my assets,
   I own nothing Wall Street admires

(I might as well admit it).
    A few things perhaps,
    but largely unredeemable.
All my holdings are in love,
    in friendship,
    in memories and discoveries
    about life.
You could say that I am glad to be alive,
    even if
    my estate
    is pure sentimentality.

Reputation?
    No man knows me or fears me
    unless, you count my friends.
And (I might as well lay it on the table)
    they own me.
    Why I'd jump to their side
    should occasion arise.
    I'd laugh,
    I'd cry,
    I'd give,
    I'd die,
        I'd hold nothing back from them.
You could say my friends own me;
    I have no regrets.

Tally the card; count the score,
the souls of two men cry out.
One owns, the other is owned.
    Who is winner?
    Are you as confused as I,
    As we watch two men
    extinguish the lights
    and go to bed?
        One face is smiling,
        and humming off key.
        The other is frightened,
        listening to silence.

Perhaps we counted wrongly?
Perhaps we didn't know soon enough

it was a different game
with different rules
and a different judge,
mounting to different and
*   very high stakes.*

May God find among us persons for turbulent times who
forcefully confront a rebellious generation so that in
those hours of midnight games we will not be found
drenched in regret, either because we didn't act or didn't
accept the words of those who did.

AXIOM FIFTEEN
**A person for turbulent times is sensitive and tender, capable of
tears when encountered by pain, poverty, and spiritual emptiness,
a person who wishes to share a truth which extends peace to a
troubled heart. This person is moved to action when opportunity
comes to relieve suffering and to break down the walls of human
alienation.**

17/ Isaiah, the comforter/
The man of fantastic expectations

A thought-starting cartoon published years ago featured
nothing but the figures of a man and woman falling
upside down through space. "Gertrude," the man was
saying, "we can't go on living like this."

One special mark of a contemplative Christian is an
enthusiastic agreement with that statement. Wherever
people are found falling through space, as it were, it is the
man or woman who knows something of the Divine
Presence who shouts out most forcefully: *We can't go on
living like this!*

That the contemplative seeks a break in the prevailing
action is not based on fear of one's personal safety, nor is it
because one dreads an interruption of one's security or
comfort. But life lived first in the presence of God is quick
to sense potential and possibility or the contrasting
tragedy of events and attitudes gone awry.

Frederick Faber—no stranger to the presence of

God—wrote endlessly of the majesty he found in his personal worship. And from that perspective of awesomeness he regularly puts his finger on the abnormal and the deviant about him in his world.

O Lord. My heart is sick,
Sick of this everlasting change;
and life runs tediously quick
through its unresting race and varied range;
Change finds no likeness to itself in Thee
And wakes no echo in Thy mute eternity.

Our civilization drifts. Indeed it does show flashes of brilliance as it discovers more and more of what nature is all about. But for all of its incredible capacity, civilization does not know much of what man is about. And because the spiritual world, where God is engaged most intimately, remains mostly in mystery, everything else will of necessity be in tragic confusion.

When the great Jewish scholar, Abraham Joshua Heschel, began his study of the prophets, he chose to do it not only because he saw it as a necessary intellectual pursuit but because he sensed that the prophets—the original contemplatives—might expose themes and forces that make a society become cohesive and productive.

In the face of the tragic failure of the modern mind, incapable of preventing its own destruction, it became clear to me that the most important philosophical problem of the twentieth century was to find a new set of presuppositions or premises, *a different way of thinking.*

That, Heschel determined, might be found in the lives of men like Isaiah. When he chose to analyze who these men were, he wrote:

The prophet was an individual who said "no" to his society, condemning its habits and assumptions, its complacency, waywardness, and syncretism. He was often compelled to proclaim the very opposite of what his heart expected.

His fundamental objective was to reconcile man and God.
Why do the two need reconciliation? Perhaps it is due to
man's false sense of sovereignty, to his abuse of freedom, to
his aggressive, sprawling pride, resenting God's
involvement in history. [*The Prophets*, Vol. 1 (New York:
Harper and Row, 1962)]

Heschel has certainly described the force that drove
Isaiah. The man who had seen the Lord had nurtured a fierce
instinct to bring his God and his people back together
again.

But such a reconciliation in which the hearts of people
are made to reopen to the loving acts of God might not
happen if a prophet spoke only in harsh and cutting tones.
If one were to close the book on Isaiah soon after reading of
his last recorded confrontation with Hezekiah, one
might conclude that contemplatives or prophets are rather
cold, always demanding, never satisfied.

Is there a soft side to a contemplative? Does one who
comes out of the heavenly Presence bring words of hope
and healing? I believe so. The contemplative is of little use
to us if he or she remains only a *commentator* and
confronter. For I believe that we need also to see the
contemplative individual so badly needed in the
turbulent eighties and nineties of our century as one who is
also a *comforter.*

One so closely allied with the heart of God must of
necessity come away with a sense of tenderness that
belongs also to God. And in a world such as ours there is a
desperate need for genuine tenderness, for hope, for
expectations that will electrify the spirit and energize and
motivate one to attempt new starts.

Robert Greenleaf recalls a story which has sprung up
around Beethoven's composition, the C# Minor Quartet,
Opus 131. When first played in Beethoven's lifetime it
appeared to be unlike anything the master had ever
written before. "Ludwig," a friend asked, "what has
happened? We don't understand you anymore."

It is reported that Beethoven replied, "I have said all
that I have to say to my contemporaries; now I am speaking
to the future."

We have seen how the contemplative looks to the future and warns of consequences. But the contemplative also looks to the future and dreams of possibilities. He knows that God will not permit history to drag on endlessly without local and universal interventions. He knows that history can change through personal and national repentance. It has happened before. It can happen as great and godly personalities arise in various generations and challenge and enlighten people with new and better ideas. It can occur through the creation of spiritual enclaves, homes and congregations, where there is the practice of a unique sort of servanthood love. And, finally, the contemplative knows from brooding on the promises of God that there can be the anticipation of a moment—a day of the Lord—when God shall directly interrupt the turbulence of history with the appearance of his glorious Son, Jesus Christ, and reconcile all things permanently unto himself.

The contemplative broods on these things, teaches these things, and—let it be underscored—works to bring about each aspect of these things. In so doing he or she proclaims and acts out a message of comfort.

How might the contemplative Christian be a comforter? First of all, simply by the way he or she lives. A quiet consistency of word and deed does more to comfort agitated individuals than almost anything I know.

A colleague of mine says of a common friend we have had for years: "When you see him coming down the hall, you know by the look on his face that the world is rightside up, at least wherever he is located." The man of which my associate speaks is a comfort simply to be near. He is in command of his world because God is in command of him. I only know a few like him.

The contemplative, secondly, brings comfort to people *in word*. As we grow older, we become increasingly aware that here and there are people whose speech is regularly marked with things we need to hear. They are dependable in their conversation because we sense that they have just recently come from the dwelling place of him who is Eternal. We recognize such people because their conversation is not shallow, does not indulge itself on petty matters of gossip or silliness. We learn that out of such a contemplative heart flows the insight we need to hear and absorb.

Recently I shared a hotel room in Thailand with Dr. Christy Wilson. We were both participants at the Consultation on World Evangelization. People from eighty countries were there. When I first checked in, I noticed that our ninth floor room opened out on the back and somewhat unattractive parking lot of the hotel rather than over-looking the magnificent Gulf of Siam. Not only did I notice our "view," I said something about it, something negative.

Dr. Wilson's immediate reply was, "Yes, I'm so glad that they gave *us* this room so that some of the Third World Christians who never get to enjoy such things could have the better view." It was a gentle reminder, its own kind of rebuke, a source of comfort. Why should I fret about a stupid matter such as a view when others would enjoy an unprecedented opportunity. I settled in to enjoy our "view." How relaxed I now was not to have a complaining spirit.

The contemplative speaks out of the wellsprings of communion with God. How comforted we all are when David shared with us his spiritual discoveries from the "green pastures" where his own soul had been restored. What he had experienced he shared with us. Now we are the blest.

But thirdly, the contemplative does more than speak and live before us. He or she acts. Having known the intimate communion of the Lord, the contemplative begins to understand people even as Christ understood them when he walked on the earth. The contemplative becomes increasingly adept not only at sensing the times of history but also the aches of human beings, the fatigue, the disappointment, the dashed hopes, the frustration and loss of belief in oneself. Like iron to a magnet, the contemplative is consistently drawn to the center of human need.

Recently I became fascinated by the work of Sister Lucy Poulin, a Carmelite nun who in 1968 moved to Orlund,

Maine, to start a hermitage for the pursuit of the
contemplative life-style. She did not remain long in the
hermitage, however, before she began to become aware of
the rural poor in that area of Maine. Soon large amounts of
Sister Lucy's time and attention were given to the
unemployed, the sick, and the discouraged.

The hard working and compassionate nun organized
co-ops for the purchasing of food and fuel; she reopened
closed factories and invited other job-producing
businesses to enter the region. Sister Lucy and her teams
organized health centers, prenatal clinics, and training
schools that would enable people to learn new skills for the
purpose of earning a living.

It would be safe to say that Sister Lucy Poulin discovered
that the genuine contemplative always brings into the
world what one has heard God say in moments of
withdrawal from the world.

Apart from his conversations with kings and common
folk, we know little about Isaiah's daily routines. But we
do have a lot of insight into the sort of things he had thought
about when *comfort* was the subject of the day. We know
that when the turbulent hour was at its darkest, he was
ready to enunciate suitable themes that would lift the
spirits of God's people and sustain them. So majestic were
the insights Isaiah revealed that it becomes impossible to
believe that he would have drawn them anywhere else but
from the heart of God.

AXIOM SIXTEEN
**A person for turbulent times sets forth to master a knowledge
of God, his acts and his attributes. For in this high pursuit is
the foundation for all the healing and redirection that humanity
will ever need.**

18/ Isaiah, the comforter/
Theme I: A great God

One of the themes of comfort Isaiah employed for the sake
of the people was that of the Being of God himself.
Perhaps at that moment when God seemed most distant to
people, it was time for Isaiah to talk about him in the
most intimate and descriptive of terms lest people forget
who he was.

Isaiah's generation and ours need at least a few people
who appreciate and can articulate with authority their
awareness of a great God. Robert Murray McCheyenne
sensed this when he wrote:

Men return again and again to the few who have
mastered the spiritual secret, whose life has been hid with
Christ in God. These are of the old time religion, hung to
the nails of the Cross.

Few Christian thinkers have made the point more clearly
than A. W. Tozer who often concerned himself with the

human tendency to ignore God, denying him the proper ascription of his true majesty. Tozer grew livid when he spoke of those who would limit God, emasculating him through ignorance or superficial thought. "God is not a comfortable old friend," he would say; "he is the everlasting Creator, the one dwelling above time and reason, uncreated and unapproachable except on his own terms." No wonder A. W. Tozer spent long periods of his day prostrate on the floor of his study in worship of his God and in intercession which he believed drew heaven's power.

In his turbulent day Isaiah was anxious to convince people that the God of Jerusalem was neither disinterested nor detached from their affairs. If he seemed absent from daily events it was because they did not seek his presence nor sense it. This is not a novel human tendency.

A few years ago I visited with a tribe of Indians in Surinam who had only recently found Christ after having lived deep in the jungle and out of touch with any sort of civilization. When I asked the Christian chief about his thoughts of God before he found out about Jesus Christ, he answered to the translator:

We were aware of only one possible God—the spirit who had made us. But we were sure he had become so disgusted with the sort of people that we were that he'd gone off and left us to fend for ourselves. We never expected to hear from him at all.

No wonder life in the jungle among these Indians dramatically changed when they learned differently. To live without a knowledge of God is a discomforting affair. The many who attempt it willfully or ignorantly are restless until they create "substitutes" or discover appropriate spiritual anesthesia which will insulate them against the reality. When Christ prepared his disciples for his departure to heaven, it is significant that he promised "I will not leave you comfortless." The comfort of the contemplative is always based on introducing the listener to God, his presence, and his mighty acts.

In Charles Schultz' cartoon "Peanuts," he once drew
Lucy and Linus at the window of their home watching
the power of a thunderstorm.

"What if it rains so hard," Lucy asked, "and the whole
world is flooded?"

The ever-calm Linus answered, "Not to worry. In Genesis,
chapter 9, verses 13 and 14, God assured Noah that
he would never again flood the entire world and the sign
of the rainbow is a reminder of his promise."

"That sure makes me feel better," a relieved Lucy said.

And Linus quietly asserted, "Sound theology has a way of
doing that."

Isaiah believed that sound theology was Jerusalem's
greatest source of comfort when history was becoming
unsound. As the "greatness" of man and the social
structures he had created seemed less and less credible, it
became time to reaffirm before people who it was that was
eternally dependable. That is no less the great challenge
of the pastor, the spiritual leader, and the head of every
Christian home today.

With this in mind, Isaiah took great pains to comfort
the people of Jerusalem with his insight into who God was
and what he was about. For example, he wanted them to
know, first of all, that the God of Jerusalem was not a silent
but a speaking God.

Comfort, comfort my people, says your God. Speak tenderly
to Jerusalem, and cry to her that her warfare is ended, that
her inquity is pardoned, that she has received from the
Lord's hand double for all her sins. [Isa. 40:1, 2]

The old contemplative craved for people to know that
the God who spoke did not always thunder forth in anger.
Tenderness could be in his voice; his was a heart of
urgency to shed grace and deliverance upon all who would
call upon his name.

We have in our living room a beautiful painting of an
Italian street scene which my wife and I purchased from
an artist in Naples several years ago. It was the old artist's
last work painted just before he had experienced a

paralyzing stroke which left his painting hand useless. Weeping, he told us of how he had gone to a church and given his last fifty dollars to the statue of his favorite saint, "But she never answered," he said. How sad a man's religion who has a god who doesn't speak.

Elijah the prophet had challenged the priests of Baal on this very issue when he faced them down before the people of Israel at the summit of Mt. Carmel. Daring them to get their god to speak or act he said:

"Cry aloud, for he is a god; either he is musing, or he has gone aside, or he is on a journey, or perhaps he is asleep and must be awakened." And they cried aloud, and cut themselves after their custom with swords and lances, until the blood gushed out upon them. And as midday passed, they raved on until the time of the offering of the oblation, but there was no voice; no one answered, no one heeded. [1 Kings 18:27-29]

Francis Schaeffer's book titled *He Is There and He Is Not Silent* (Wheaton, IL: Tyndale, 1972) is all the slogan the contemporary Christian needs to initially proclaim to the discomforted person. He is not silent, and when he speaks, he can speak tenderly.

Isaiah's spiritual communion with heaven also brought the information that the God of Jerusalem could be an *involved* and *interacting* God:

Behold, the Lord God comes with might, and his arm rules for him; behold, his reward is with him, and his recompense before him.

He will feed his flock like a shepherd, he will gather the lambs in his arms, he will carry them in his bosom, and gently lead those that are with young. [Isa. 40:10, 11]

The contemplative wanted his people to know that God could enter their midst as a conquering general, pacifying a rebellious city, or he could come as a tender shepherd, feeding and protecting all of those who sought to yield to his care. What incredible contrasts: a shepherd and a general.

What an incredible God who does not stalk off in disgust, abandoning his people to their own ends. He chooses to identify with all whom he has made.

Isaiah also desired that Jerusalem know that there was a *generous* God. Perhaps they could be comforted by such words as:

[God] gives power to the faint, and to him who has no might he increases strength. Even youths shall faint and be weary, and young men shall fall exhausted; but they who wait for the Lord shall renew their strength, they shall mount up with wings as eagles, they shall run and not be weary, they shall walk and not faint. [Isa. 40:29-31]

For the spiritually troubled and hungry, for the exhausted of spirit and the broken heart, Isaiah's words must have been a special morale booster. This was no selfish God; he was generous, gracious, willing to give to those whose fists became unclenched, whose tired arms reached out to receive.

Isaiah's God was a *choosing* God also. He wanted the people of Jerusalem to think on the fact that they were divinely selected to be his children. A mystery, to say the least, but an important one.

I have chosen you and not cast you off; fear not, for I am with you, be not dismayed, for I am your God; I will strengthen you, I will help you, I will uphold you with my victorious right hand. [Isa. 41:9, 10]

In my college days I worked as a clerk in a trucking company. It was a common task to walk the loading dock collecting bills of lading from each doorway where truck trailers were taking on freight. All about were the large crates and boxes, often marked with the familiar "Fragile—handle with care."

Perhaps it was that memory that caused me to be all the more amused when I recently saw a cartoon in which a forklift operator approached a similar large crate to pick it up. But his face reflected confusion as he read on the side of the box, "Contents unknown—handle with nonchalance."

To the God of Jerusalem, the contents of the people were not unknown. His inclination toward them was not one of nonchalance but of deliberate sovereign choice and intimate involvement. They were not pawns in history but rather, as many of us used to sing, "precious jewels." In a turbulent hour when choices-turned-into-consequences were breaking out all about them, these were comforting words to hear.

It was no trivial matter that God called Jerusalem's people his children. There was comfort in knowing that God was father to all who would accept the loving embrace of his family experience.

I will say to the north, Give up, and to the south, Do not withhold; bring my sons from afar and my daughters from the end of the earth, every one who is called by my name, whom I created for my glory, whom I formed and made. [Isa. 43:6, 7]

My friend Stanley Mooneyham tells the story of a family where, in years past, it was a tradition for each of the children in his or her turn to go out the front door and bring in the milk when it was delivered by the milkman early in the morning. That certainly dates the story. In the dead of winter early one of those mornings when the days were shortened and it was quite dark, it was the turn of the youngest boy in the family to do the milk chore. Mooneyham reports that the child opened the door, cautiously looked out into the dark, and then shut it quickly saying, "It's much too dark for a boy to go out there without a father."

Jerusalem badly needed a father also—a heavenly one. It was too dark a time in their history to go long without one. And part of the message of Isaiah was to remind people that they had just that: a Father who had chosen them and wanted to back them up with eternal strength. Some certainly must have been comforted in that fact.

When the contemporary congregation meets weekly for worship, we should not ignore the significance of the

beginning of the Lord's prayer, "Our Father. . . ." In this
simple identification he has told us the kind of
relationship he seeks also to establish with us. As it was
once in Jerusalem, so the same comfort is available today.

When Isaiah wanted to comfort the people of Jerusalem
by sharing with them his discoveries of the nature of
God, he also lingered upon the great fact that God's *power*
was utterly dependable and consistent.

Fear not, for I have redeemed you; I have called you by
name, you are mine. When you pass through the waters I
will be with you; and through the rivers, they shall not
overwhelm you; when you walk through fire you shall not
be burned, and the flames shall not consume you . . .
because you are precious in my eyes . . . and I love you. [Isa.
43:1-4]

These are incredible revelations of a personal God.
Only one who had spent long periods of time in meditation
and communion with the God of Jerusalem could have so
beautifully expressed dimensions of deity that hardly
anyone else knew about. Just as Isaiah had been careful to
expose to Jerusalem the anger of a just and wrathful God, he
was now careful to draw upon the same spiritual resource
to comfort them with portraits of a Lord who did indeed
love them. As a pastor and spiritual leader, I am
prompted by Isaiah to realize that the people under my care
need regularly to hear about this aspect of God.

A midwest pastor friend of mine once told of going out to
a home to call upon a family who regularly attended his
church. The front yard of the home was closed off by a fence
and a gate. When he arrived a small girl was playing alone
by the front steps of the home. Seeing the pastor get out of
his car, she immediately ran up the steps and shouted
through the screen door, "Mommy, mommy, the angry man
who shouts a lot is here."

My friend accepted the incident as a subtle reminder
that people do not always need the angry shouts of one
who wants to reflect the wrath of God. They need also the
tender affirmations of one who has been in the presence

of a good God who wants his people also to know that "they are precious in my eyes, and honored, and I love you. . . ."

An evening at Fenway Park, the home of the Boston Red Sox, might send most people home in either delirium or depression, depending how you feel about our mercurial home team. In my case, I returned home one night to write the following piece of reflective poetry.

I came to cheer one night in a baseball park
where banks of arc lights turned the
sky's darkness into artificial sky.

In that stadium filled crowds to SRO,
I watched the greatest names in baseball
pitch, hit, and catch a simple, small,
round ball.

And a crowd of thousands and thousands,
writhing in enthusiasm,
absorbed in expentancy,
burst with frenzied emotion,
at the slightest motion of any famed athlete.

So tense was the drama, that it seemed for a moment,
if there were no further perimeter
to the real world,
except the top row of bleachers
where cold beer flowed like a small river
and smoke rose like incense on a pagan altar.

To hear the prejudice of the crowd,
it seemed as if the greatest human beings
in history stood in the batter's box
or on the pitcher's mound.

To sense the tenseness of the tie score,
in the 9th inning, it seemed
as no other event in the years
of humankind came near to the significance
of this exchange
between a man on the mound
and another at bat.

But as I sat, faintly tempted to abandon myself
  to this twisted view of reality,
  I caught from the corner of my eye,
  just beyond the glare of the leftfield lights,
  a tiny sparkling star.

Its tiny spark, its remote position
  made it seem as if it had nothing to do with,
  or to say, concerning the pandemonium
  within that athletic temple.

But I strained to listen with the ears of my
  spirit and suddenly heard what no one
  else could hear.

The star, a still small voice whispered,
  had been there in the sky longer and
  longer than the oldest stadium.
It had burned light-years before the game of
  baseball had been conceived.
It would burn long after mighty Casey
  would strike out . . . even retire with pension
  to oblivion.
And it would point to the God whose
  moves in time and space are far greater
  than the foolish efforts of a fearsome slugger
  about whom thousands presently scream.

Why do men choose to see and hear the trivial
  efforts of something just a game,
  yet miss the chance to stand in awe
  of a star, twinkling just beyond the
  floodlights,
  whose magnitude is ten times greater than
  our sun?

Why do we reverse the scale of events,
  making the shorter the longer,
  the bigger the smaller,
  the insignificant the more prominent?

It is a mystery:
  but until it is solved,

the tiny, quiet star will go on twinkling,
just beyond the arc lights,
telling anyone who will stop and listen
that God is there,
and that the times of history are in his hand.

A reflection upon Isaiah's sound theology about a great God has to raise a number of questions in my mind about the direction of our theology today. Does contemporary preaching regularly reflect themes regarding the incomparable nature of God? Or has the pursuit of theology become so utterly a professional and purely intellectual exercise that these great sources of comfort and stability get lost in the jargons and game-playing of the classroom of the graduate school?

What do we teach our children about God? What is the content of many modern Christian songs and testimonies that reduce the Ruler of heaven to the role of a celestial Santa Claus or "the Man Upstairs." There is no comfort in such an insipid God as many see him today.

If our faith is to be resolute and strong there must be those who will tell us the truth about this one who is above all. They must bring to bear every resource at their disposal to bless us with the news of his Being, and his mighty acts, and our resulting comfort will be that which is not built on escape or naiveté but of confidence that when the game of history has reached its conclusion, it will be clear to all men (rebel or servant) that our God, the great God of Jerusalem, reigns.

"You are my witnesses," says the Lord, "and my servant whom I have chosen, that you may know and believe me and understand that I am He. Before me no god was formed, nor shall there be any after me. I, I am the Lord, and besides me there is no savior." [Isa. 43:10, 11]

AXIOM SEVENTEEN
A person for turbulent times lives in the expectation of a "day"
when God will bring the turbulence of history to a
conclusion and set in motion a new order of work and
relationship, of wholeness and worship. Certain of this
promised moment, such a person settles the troubled spirits
of those who formerly were convinced of the inevitability of
chaos.

19/ Isaiah, the comforter/ Theme II: A great day

Isaiah not only loved to reflect the good news about an
immense and loving God, but when comforting people,
he brought a second major theme to bear. That was the
theme of a great day of change coming. "Behold, I am doing a
new thing; now it springs forth, do you not perceive it?"
(Isa. 43:19).

Isaiah believed in the doctrine of "days" and beyond that
of a great culminating day. The history of the people of
God was replete with special days when God had
intervened and upset the natural progression of things in
order to defend his people. The greatest day of all in the past,
of course, had been that of the Exodus, when God had not
only staged the release of his people from the bondage of
Pharaoh, but caused the Egyptians to send the Hebrews
off with provisions and possessions. Through the centuries
the people had never forgotten the unprecedented night of
the Exodus when God's power had overcome the greatest
human power of the known world.

There had been other turbulent "days" when God had
shown his faithfulness. When things had seemed bleak in
the face of the marauding Philistines, God had raised up a
young boy, David, equipped him with a ridiculous
slingshot, and used him to silence Goliath and send his
people into headlong retreat.

Just when things were the darkest, Isaiah would comfort
his people with reminders that there was coming an even
greater day. "A new thing would happen, and all of nature
would reflect the changed order."

The Lord of hosts has a day against all that is proud and
lofty, against all that is lifted up and high; against the
Cedars of Lebanon . . . against all the high mountains . . .
against every high tower . . . against all the ships of
Tarshish. . . . And the haughtiness of man shall be
humbled, and the pride of men shall be brought low. . . . And
the idols shall utterly pass away. And men shall enter the
caves of the rocks . . . from before the terror of the Lord, and
from the glory of his majesty, when he rises to terrify the
earth. [Isa. 2:12-19]

My father used to love to share the story of a man passing
by a neighborhood baseball game where young boys clad
in uniforms much too big for them were earnestly imitating
their big league heroes. "What's the score?" he called to
the third baseman. "30-0 their favor," the boy responded,
"but we haven't had our ups yet."

Isaiah would have liked the story if he had understood
baseball, because it illustrated the point he had often
tried to make to those in need of comfort. One can almost
hear him saying, "God hasn't come to bat yet, and when
he does, he'll blow history's game wide open."

The Lord has a day for those who are faithful and a day
for those who are wrathful. And when the changes have
taken place, a magnificent tranquility will ensue. There
will be a new beauty to public and private worship.

It shall come to pass in the latter days that the mountain of
the house of the Lord shall be established as the highest

of the mountains, and shall be raised above the hills; and all the nations shall flow to it, and many peoples shall come and say: "Come, let us go up to the mountain of the Lord, to the house of the God of Jacob; that he may teach us his ways and that we may walk in his paths." [Isa. 2:2, 3]

Isaiah's scenario of the future must have confounded those who heard it. The prophet had brought from his meditation the picture of an entire world making a pilgrimage to Jerusalem, not to plunder its gold, but to draw from its experience of worship and its knowledge of Jehovah. Was there any more marvelous opportunity than that of unfolding the righteousness of God to those who would say "teach us?"

The theme of the great day held comfort for all those who had known nothing but the turbulence of war and its hateful effects. The fact was, Isaiah proclaimed, that when God intervened, the priorities and pursuits of people would change.

They shall beat their swords into plowshares, and their spears into pruning hooks; nation shall not lift up sword against nation, neither shall they learn war any more. [2:4]

Students of Scripture may often disagree about the exact time and order of the events of the great day, but all agree that we may anticipate a coming time when a new structure of life will be pressed into history. God's faithful ones will be vindicated; justice will be fulfilled and the potential of creation will be realized to proclaim the glory of God. Heaven's enemies will be pacified and all will call Israel's God, Lord.

To this day many of us yearn for Isaiah's comforting dream. As those who contemplate the nature and work of God, we too ask, "Lord, how long? When shall these things be? When shall the leaders of the earth finally come to grips with the insanity of brutality and hostility? When shall the refugees be permitted to go home, those unjustly in prison released to families, the child able to eat?" So inept is the human race to bring such things about under its own power, we must pray that the great day will be hastened along by a God who one day will ultimately bring a change that will last for eternity. Already in his time Isaiah contemplated and expected that to happen.

I fully believe that until that day arrives, it is the responsibility of the community of Christ, the great church of our generation, to pursue that dream and the power of God's Holy Spirit.

Henry Nouwen writes:

It is in the midst of this dark world that the Christian community is being tested. Can we be light, salt, and leaven to our brothers and sisters in the human family? Can we offer hope, courage, and confidence to the people of this era? Can we break through the paralyzing fear by making those who watch us exclaim, "See, how they love one another, how they serve their neighbor, and how they pray to their Lord?" Or do we have to confess that at this juncture of history we just do not have that needed strength of the generosity and that our Christian communities are little more than sodalities of well-intentioned people supporting each other and their individual interests? [*Clowning in Rome* (Garden City, NY: Doubleday, 1979)]

Until that great day which Isaiah expected, it is we in the name of our God who should live as if change has already come. For indeed it has already come in our hearts if Jesus Christ is Lord. This I hold to be an indisputable fact leading to an exciting possibility.

AXIOM EIGHTEEN
A person for turbulent times joyfully accepts the invitation of
Jesus to become conformed to his divine personhood. This
person shares this choice with others to the end that they also
might make a similar decision and also find a possibility for
wholeness.

20/ Isaiah, the comforter/ Theme III: A great revelation

It is reasonable to assume that the temple in Jerusalem was
jammed with people on all sorts of errands the day an old
man named Simeon spied a young couple making their way
through the temple gate with a newborn child. Simeon,
too, was of the contemplative tradition, for of him it is
said, "... this man was righteous and devout, looking for the
consolation of Israel."

Years spent in the acts of worship and meditation had
sensitized old Simeon to divine matters of which no one else
would have been aware, and that is why only he and a
woman of similar discipline, Anna, approached the obscure
couple with a wish to embrace their child and extend to
it a blessing. While holding it, Simeon said:

Lord, now lettest thou thy servant depart in peace,
according to thy word; for mine eyes have seen thy
salvation which thou has prepared in the presence of all
peoples, a light for revelation to the Gentiles, and for
glory to thy people Israel. [Luke 2:29-32]

In such a strange encounter—which no one else probably noticed—an old man and woman were comforted. Unlike anyone in the great religious center, they knew what was happening. A "light" was beginning to glow, and they were enriched by the realization that when its illumination reached peak candlepower, all Gentiles and Jews alike would know that God was keeping promises made centuries before through Isaiah and others like him.

A great revelation was underway. This time it was not simply the announcement of facts and statements about God. And this time it was not even one more mysterious supernatural intervention when all human resources had been exhausted on a battlefield or during an epidemic. But this time heaven would speak through a person, a child who would grow to be about his Father's business. And when the child-become-man had finished his work, "the thoughts of many hearts [would] be revealed."

What Simeon held in his arms, Isaiah spoke about in mysterious terms centuries before:

The people . . . in darkness have seen a great light. [Isa. 9:2]

Ho, every one who thirsts, come to the waters; and he who has no money, come, buy and eat! Come, buy wine and milk without money and without price. [Isa. 55:1]

To the people who heard Isaiah utter such declarations and invitations, there must have been an odd mixture of tranquility and confusion. Whatever was he trying to say? Perhaps Isaiah himself was not always absolutely sure. Peter acknowledged that it was quite possible that the contemplative prophets of the Old Testament often possessed senses of certain truths but not a full understanding of all of them.

The prophets who prophesied of the grace that was to be yours searched and inquired about this salvation; they inquired what person or time was indicated by the Spirit of Christ within them when predicting the sufferings of Christ and the subsequent glory. It was revealed to them that they were serving not themselves but you, in the things which have now been announced . . . . [1 Peter 1:10-12]

So it should not surprise us if Isaiah did not fully understand the entire future implication of all that God had whispered into his heart. But one thing is sure, Isaiah had no doubt that the great consolation of which Simeon later spoke was a person, Immanuel, meaning God is with us.

Threaded throughout the lifetime of Isaiah's words are constant references to his unbridled belief and expectation of the revelation of such a person, the Author of an eternal heart-resting comfort. And what were the things that Isaiah anticipated?

He had no doubt, first of all, that this special revelation of God would ultimately consolidate all power under himself. The confusing international power struggle that was forever going on would be subdued. This coming One would be Lord of all the nations.

Of the increase of his government and of peace there will be no end, upon the throne of David, and over his kingdom, to establish it, and to uphold it with justice and with righteousness from this time forth and for evermore. The zeal of the Lord of hosts will do this. [Isa. 9:7]

In a city that was beginning to watch a succession of kings who waffled on the truth, who tried to play up to foreign powers, who caved in at the slightest hint of pressure, Isaiah's description of this coming King must have been great news.

Add to that Isaiah's profound conviction that the special One to come would clean up life in the streets of Jerusalem and in other places.

I have put my spirit upon him, he will bring forth justice to the nations . . . he will not fail or be discouraged till he has established justice in the earth; and the coastlands wait for his law.

If one is used to being kicked around, exploited, discriminated against, Isaiah's words are indeed good news.

His God was a God of justice, and when the grand
moment of his revelation came, wrongs would be righted,
and "hidden things would be brought to light."

When men come out of the presence of God impressed
with the things that concern God, justice emerges as a
great convicting theme. Is anything being revealed if it
becomes apparent that the subject of justice is all too
often ignored by many kinds of Christians today? Why do
the contemplative prophets of the Bible reserve their
anger for those who have subverted justice? And why do
they spare their compassion for those who have suffered
because of injustice? Can any gospel—the sort being
preached then or now—really reflect the Being of God and
his comforting hand if it ignores the element of justice?

When justice is proclaimed and demanded, some
people end up gaining what God meant to be rightfully
theirs, while others are compelled to give up that which
they gained unjustly. Take Zacchaeus, for example. Visited
by Jesus Christ, his overall financial statement quickly
suffered enormous losses while those of people in his
neighborhood suddenly swelled. What was said over that
dinner table that compelled a voluntary shifting of large
amounts of money? The subject of justice had to be part
of that conversation.

For the poor, for the disadvantaged, for the suffering, for
the frightened, Isaiah's comforting message that someone
was coming who would make right their lossees must
have been beautiful news. They had looked again and again
to Jerusalem's religious establishment and come away let
down and betrayed. There had been no comforting
consolation there. Isaiah looked at this source of their
distress and said,

Is not this the fast [true worship] that I choose; to loose the
bonds of wickedness, to undo the thongs of the yoke, to
let the oppressed go free, and to break every yoke? Is it not to
share your bread with the hungry, and bring the homeless
poor into your house; when you see the naked, to cover
him, and not to hide yourself from your own flesh? Then
shall your light break forth like the dawn, and your healing

shall spring up speedily. . . . Then you shall call, and the
Lord will answer; you shall cry, and he will say, Here I am.
[Isa. 58:6-9]

What a change would take place when this one came in
the name of the Lord and said as God's anointed one, "Here
I am."

Isaiah's contemplative vision of change began to take
shape in living color several centuries later when one day
a young man, age thirty, familiar to most as the son of
Joseph the carpenter, entered the Nazareth synagogue,
took the scrolls from the attendant, and read a portion from
the old prophet himself.

The Spirit of the Lord God is upon me, because the Lord
has anointed me to bring good tidings to the afflicted; he has
sent me to bind up the broken-hearted, to proclaim
liberty to the captives, and the opening of the prison to
those who are bound; to proclaim the year of the Lord's
favor. [Isa. 61:1, 2]

Closing the book at that point—deliberately
interrupting the full text of the reading—the young man
sat down, as preachers of that day did, and said: "Today this
Scripture has been fulfilled in your hearing."

The congregation was absolutely stunned. They knew
exactly what Jesus was saying. The "acceptable year of
the Lord" was the code-phrase for change. Everyone
understood it. If the day of the Lord spoke of God's
intervention from without in order to rescue Israel from its
enemies and its spiritual rebellion, the "acceptable year
of the Lord" spoke of a reordering of structures and
relationships from within. For those in debt, those
enslaved, those staggering under the enormous weight of
the momentum of failure, the acceptable year of the Lord
meant the possibility of a new start. There was potential for
liberation from one's past.

The life and work of Jesus Christ cannot be understood
apart from that stirring announcement. His agenda came
straight out of Isaiah's dream which, of course, had been

born in the prophet's own touch with God. This was the liberating Christ, the Christ of new starts and new opportunities, God with us.

The potential of new starts was on my mind when a couple came to visit with me in my study. They share a second marriage, several children from each other's past marriages, and a string of conflicts and hurts that now threaten to split them apart. Their home is marked with turbulence. On the weekend previous to our meeting, the husband had stalked out of the house in total frustration. It had been a long Friday night, Saturday, and Sunday morning until he returned, expecting that he would find his wife gone, the house vacated.

At that point his wife picked up the story. She had indeed planned to leave but kept putting off the inevitable first steps. On Saturday morning, wandering around the quiet house, she had reached for a book on the shelf that she had recently purchased at a book party. Now I understood why they had come to see me since I was the author of the book and it was on marriage (what pride I might have had, however, was quickly diminished when she laughingly explained that the color of the cover caused her choice since it matched her living room decor).

The first pages had caught her attention, she said, and she went on to read the entire book (my author's pride was salvaged). For her the book seemed to pinpoint some of the reasons behind the marital struggles of her home. She determined to give her marriage another chance and so she waited for her husband to return.

As they continued the description of the weekend, he spoke of his surprise and cautious delight that she was still there when he came back. He detailed for me their ensuing conversation, her report of what she learned from the book, and their decision to get in touch with me. What they sought was not answers to their problems, he said. They thought they knew about those. But the real question was in the will and power to change habit and personality patterns that ambush the relationship and defeat it. What hope was there for change they asked, before it was too late?

I would have had nothing for them had Christ never quoted and implemented the comforting words of Isaiah. "The acceptable year of the Lord" is a message that is not only economic in perspective but spiritual. To follow Christ, I told them, is to realize a new power within that invites extraordinary change. It rebukes old ways and follows new ones. It creates new tastes and new aspirations. But a choice must be made to accept this brand of comfort. Many, I warned them, have not. In my mind I recall that the people of Nazareth didn't, and Mark would later record that, "Christ could do no mighty works there because of their unbelief."

But unlike the citizens of Nazareth, this couple were drawn to the comfort that Christ presents—that of the possibility of change—and they asked me what to do. Soon they knelt as an act of submission and were asking Christ to enter their lives and create "an acceptable year" for their marriage. He did, and the last few years of their marriage prove that. Remarkable changes have taken place in their home. Isaiah would enjoy meeting my friends whose lives have been marked with the sort of change he believed in when he comforted the people of his time.

But, as Nazareth certainly demonstrated, not everyone was ready to embrace the comfort that Isaiah anticipated and Christ embodied. As John would later write, "He came to his own home, and his own people received him not" (John 1:11). As once it had been with Ahaz, much of Israel wasn't buying in Christ's day either. The revelation of God was to be rejected by most. Had the contemplative sensed that possibility centuries before also when he wrote,

He was despised and rejected by men; a man of sorrows, acquainted with grief; and as one from whom men hide their faces he was despised, and we esteemed him not. [Isa. 53:3]

Did Isaiah ever become inwardly enraged over the seeming confusion of his own meditations as he contemplated what God was saying in his heart? Did he ever make sense out of the apparent contradictions as he prophetically thought over One who was at once a champion of justice and salvation while at the same time was also being "oppressed and afflicted." Could he reconcile the images of a conquering king and the pathetic picture of a bleeding lamb? Although he might not fully comprehend it, all of this he proclaimed with a confidence that God would bring it to pass in a way that would uphold his glory.

What did Isaiah understand about the coming Anointed One in relationship to the atonement of the cross? Could the old contemplative have fully perceived what it meant when he wrote, "The Lord would lay upon him the sins of us all"? For comfort means not only a conquering crown but an ugly cross. Isaiah had called to the people of Jerusalem to prepare for the coming of the Lord, Christ.

In the wilderness prepare the way of the Lord, make straight in the desert a highway for our God. Every valley shall be lifted up, and every mountain and hill be made low; the uneven ground shall become level, and the rough places a plain. And the glory of the Lord shall be revealed, and all flesh shall see it together, for the mouth of the Lord has spoken. [Isa. 40:3-5]

Perhaps Isaiah did not fully realize that the road prepared through the wilderness would lead straight over Calvary and that that part of the victory involved preliminary rejection, crucifixion, and burial. It shouldn't surprise us that Isaiah might not have fully comprehended all of this. The disciples didn't either just months before Jesus told them it was about to happen.

But the fact was that:

He was wounded for our transgressions, he was bruised for our iniquities; upon him was the chastisement that made us whole, and with his stripes we are healed. [Isa. 53:5]

What Jesus Christ accomplished at the cross paved the way for the realization of all Isaiah's dreams. In dying he took upon himself the sins of the world. In resurrection he focused on the way and method by which Isaiah's dreams of change and peace would take place.

And so this was part of Isaiah's offer of comfort to the people of his time, and even though they would not be able to understand the full chronology of these strange matters, they could be comforted in the fact that God was active and alive on their behalf. He would not abandon them. He was indeed coming, and that might be all they would need to know.

Arnold Prater recalls:

. . . a man I knew who stood behind the second chair in a barber shop where I was a customer. The owner of the shop was a friend of mine, but this fellow in the second chair, a man who was about sixty-five years of age, was about the vilest, most vulgar, profane, wicked-talking man I had ever known. He must have had some kind of fixation about preachers for it seemed to me that every time I entered the shop he doubled his output.

One day when I went in he was gone. I asked my friend where he was, and my friend said, "Oh, he's been desperately ill. And for awhile they despaired of his life."

Perhaps six weeks after that, as I was entering the post office one day, I heard a voice call my name. I turned and saw the profane man. He was seated in a car so he could watch the people pass. He was a mere shadow of a man and his face was the color of death itself.

He crooked a bony finger at me and I walked over to where he was. He said, in a voice so weak I had to lean forward to catch the words, "Preacher, I want to tell you something."

Then he went on, "I was in a coma down there in the hospital. I could not move nor see. They did not know it, but I could still hear, and I heard the doctor tell my wife, 'I don't think he can last another hour.'

Then his voice trembled so it was a moment before he could continue. "Preacher," he said, "I had never prayed in

my entire lifetime, but I prayed then. I said, 'O God, if
there is a God, I need you now!' And when I said that . . . I
—I don't know how to put it into words, but all I can say
is—I was given an assurance that He was there."

Then the tears welled up in his reddened eyes and he said,
"Oh, preacher, just imagine! I've kicked him in the face
every day of my life for sixty years, and the first time I
call His name—*He came.*" [*Release from Phoniness* (Waco,
TX: Word, 1968)]

In a cartoon a man and a woman fall upside down through
space and realize that they cannot go on living like
this. So the contemplative prophet—Isaiah—commentator,
confronter, and comforter—knew that his turbulent
world could not go on much longer either. There would
either be repentance and salvation or increasing
resistance and judgment. Those were the choices, and those
were the consequences.

I marvel at Isaiah, at his resilience and his courage to
stand alone in turbulent times saying those things, whose
authority was based solely on the quality of his walk with
God. Could he survive today? Or would his voice be
drowned in the clamor for statistics, footnotes and
documentation, connections and even laughs? Is there a
place any longer for the person whose unquestioned
authority is founded on the vigor of his spiritual power
rooted in meditation and the contemplative disciplines?

William Barclay wrote,

In the old days, when much of the world was unexplored
and unknown, and when many lands were lands of
mystery, men drew their maps; and in the unknown places
they wrote such things as "Here be dragons" or "Here be
burning, fiery sands." The Christian can take the map of
life and write across every part of it "Here is Christ."
[*Letters To the Seven Churches* (Nashville: Abingdon,
n.d.)]

The Jerusalem of Uzziah, Jotham, Ahaz, and Hezekiah
needed a man who could point to the map and say just that:

Here is the Anointed One; here is the Christ. That person needed to be one who could say it in a form of commentary, confrontation, or comfort. In that day the person for turbulent times was Isaiah, the contemplative. Today he needs to be found in homes, in churches, in the streets of our own cities. Where is he?

PART FOUR
EPILOGUE

AXIOM NINETEEN
A person for turbulent times accepts the call to be an agent for God and his truth within the home, the neighborhood, the congregation, the circle of work, and the nation. From such people who will pay the supreme price comes hope for the future and the possibility of peace today.

21/ Wanted: A person for turbulent times

When I leave my home in Lexington, Massachusetts, to drive to the airport in Boston, I take a route that passes by the reservoir in Stoneham on Interstate 93. Usually it is a magnificent sight and causes one to rejoice all the more over the beautiful countryside that God has given to those of us who live in New England.

Recently, the people in Stoneham drained the reservoir and a lovely pond turned into a muddy, unsightly bog. The water had covered up so many things I hadn't known about. On the bottom were tree stumps, all sorts of garbage and waste, and a lot of plant growth that was anything but indicative of the beauty I'm used to seeing on my way to the airport.

As I pondered the ugliness of the empty Stoneham reservoir it occurred to me that a person, a family, a church, and even a society can become like that. As long as there are resources, a cover-up can be arranged that makes an ugly piece of life-style look in fact as if it's quite beautiful. But lower the level of the "cover-up" and the sight is frighteningly different.

The pharaoh of Egypt had appeared unassailable in his power until an uninterpretable dream destroyed his confidence. Uzziah, king of Jerusalem, had put together an unbeatable combination of leadership characteristics which were suddenly betrayed by the inward cancer of pride. Ahaz looked strong on paper as long as he beat a path to the Assyrian king's door, and Hezekiah looked successful the day he welcomed the Babylonians into his treasuries. But all of these men took on totally different appearances when the level of life was lowered and they appeared as they actually were.

We have less than twenty years in our world before the beginning of a brand new century. There are many signs all about us that the level of our resources is lowering to such an extent that before we reach that point of time, history may reveal that what is really underneath is not too attractive either.

To comment upon prospects for the future is a very complicated matter. Many Christians, of course, believe that there is probably not going to be a future, that the return of Isaiah's anticipated Messiah is just around the corner. There is certainly much in the prophetic passages to support their expectations. But I am not comfortable with that one single perspective, for the Christ who said "be ye ready" also indicated that we should "occupy until I come."

Those who have chosen the life-style and faith of a Christian must take another look at this world. Two prevailing Christian perspectives among evangelicals are, first, those who have so entirely embraced prophetic predictions, that they are prepared to abandon this world at the first sign of rapture. They tend to think like those who once lived in a town in Maine who were told that within two years their community would be inundated by the rising waters of a dammed up river. The people simply lost interest in maintaining their homes and their property. Soon a once beautiful community became a virtual slum. They anticipated no tomorrow; therefore they sat back and simply absorbed the daily reports of the rising water level.

Another view—commendable to be sure, but somewhat inadequate also—is that of those whose only desire is to "evangelize" the world. For these well-meaning Christians, it seems enough to confront people with the substance of the sinners' prayer and then hope for the best. For many years I have listened to the argument that if enough people were converted in a society, they would infect that society with righteousness.

More than one out of every five Americans claim a born-again experience, but these observations suggest to me that converted Americans have not made a substantial impact upon America. I grant that this is difficult to measure, but I will stick to the notion that evangelism, while the primary task of Christians, is not the only task of Christians.

No, there is a third possible perspective for Christians in this world and, in part, I draw precedence for this posture from the two men this book has highlighted: Joseph and Isaiah.

This third view of our world suggests that some day it will indeed be abandoned for a new one. Furthermore, it agrees that people need to be confronted with the saving gospel of Jesus Christ in every way that we can get out the good news. But add to those two convictions the realization that we must also redeem all of *today* as long as God judges history worthy of continued existence.

The world may endure for a thousand or more years. That we see signs of a decay and disintegration does not presuppose an end to all things. Perhaps it means the decline of one or more of a chain of civilizations that the God of history has permitted to come and go. We can't be sure, and we exhaust our energies if we continually debate that point. The real issue is today and what we're going to do with it.

A "Joseph" brings leadership to a turbulent today. He shapes things in his own personal world. He stamps whatever he touches with the character of God. A host of Josephs could go a long way to resolving and redeeming many of the dilemmas we face in our generation. Josephs would have a lot to say about the ethics of taking human life, the criteria behind business decisions, the morality by which governments are conducted. Josephs might be laughed at on occasions, and they would certainly know criticism and attack when they made mistakes or pursued decisions that would only be vindicated in the future. But nevertheless Josephs could make a great difference.

Alongside of the Josephs with bold leadership must come the perceptive Isaiahs who can help us see ourselves and our God. These contemplatives can sharpen our spiritual senses as they show us new ways of looking at old things and old ways of looking at new things. They can teach us how to reemploy the full range of our emotions, moving from the exercise of righteous anger to unbridled joy and praise.

In contrast we are all too often confronted with Christians who in frustration take the easy way out saying nothing or assuming that they are not responsible. I am reminded of the voice of Mr. Common-man in the play *A Man for All Seasons.* Sir Thomas More has been executed by the king for his convictions. Common-man has remained uninvolved, taking no sides. And after the bloody deed is done, he says,

I'm breathing . . . are you breathing too? It's nice isn't it? It isn't so difficult to keep alive, friends—just don't make trouble—or if you must make trouble, make the sort of trouble that's expected. Well, I don't need to tell you that . . .

A slow-motion replay of the lives and work of Joseph and Isaiah strongly suggests that the sort of "trouble" they got into did indeed go to the roots of the worlds in which they lived. Their time and interest was not expended on matters about which people had no care

Joseph was willing to blow the whistle on the shoddy business practices of his brothers. He drew the line on moral

choices. He possessed impeccable integrity in running a
nation. Isaiah, on the other hand, was not overwhelmed by
the opinions of the religious establishment. He was not
intimidated by the office of the king when it came time to
tell him that his foreign policy was spineless. And he did
not flinch when he posed that stunning question to
Hezekiah, "What did they see in your house?"

You could say that our Lord was not afraid of trouble
either. It wasn't that he was a trouble-maker—although
some did call him that—but rather that his positions, his
insights, and his actions pointed to where there was
trouble all too often covered up and made beautiful in the
same way the Stoneham reservoir appears to be beautiful.
You can almost hear the Savior walking into situations
made acceptable by most over the years and saying,
"Let's lower the level just a bit and see what's really there."
All too often the real heart of the oppressor, the greedy,
the power-hungry, the proud was exposed in its ugliness.

If Isaiah and Joseph walked through our turbulent
world, what do you suppose might concern them? Perhaps
the list would go on and on. But stop and ask yourself:
With what would a leader with authentic charisma and a
holy man with contemplative instincts concern
themselves?

On a national and international level I suspect that they
would have brought insight and direction to bear on a host
of mind-boggling matters: the issues of peace and war,
the support of governments committed to basic human
rights, the pursuit of policies that bring back refugees to
their homes, food to starving people, and liberation for
those who are oppressed. Would they have been shocked
to discover that these Christian concerns and values are
often ignored or unmentioned among many people who
claim to follow Christ today?

And what might the two men say if they were to walk our
city streets? Would they take time to muse and act upon
the unavoidable reality of the poor? Would they show care
for the person in a penal system who slowly sinks into
depression or bitterness because of neglect? And what might

their reaction be over the toleration of crime in neighborhoods where people do not possess political clout at city hall?

What would a Joseph say about politicians on the take or an Isaiah about entertainers entering our homes through television with humor and drama that is hardly above alley cat morality? Would Joseph with his managerial acumen have anything to say to a boss or a board of directors about the nature of corporate objectives if they pivoted only upon profit and ignored the human development of both employee and customer? Might Isaiah bring comment to bear upon the tragic loss of a day of rest in America when people could break the tyrannic bonds of work and acquisition and worship their God?

You have to wonder if Joseph and Isaiah wouldn't have been shocked over the turbulent state of affairs in the American family, our view of the preciousness of life in matters such as abortion, or the plight of the elderly.

Each of us could compile an exhaustive list of issues and concerns being discovered as the level of life in Western society seems to lower. My list hardly scratches the surface. It only represents things that Christians might find worth thinking about.

But in fact, one of the greatest detriments to doing anything today is the feeling that the needs and dilemmas of our generation are so enormous that intended action gives way to paralysis, as we choose to do nothing. There is so much for the Christian to accomplish that perhaps the easiest thing is to ignore it all. Fortunately, neither Isaiah nor Joseph fell for that sort of thinking.

I continue to be an absolute optimist about the future. But my optimism is predicated on the awakening of the Christian community to the power and wisdom available when people move forward in the name of Jesus Christ. Idealism to be sure. But Joseph was an idealist; so was Isaiah. And so was virtually every man or woman down through the centuries who made a deposit of witness and leadership within his or her generation.

The twentieth-century martyr, Bonhoeffer, was an idealist and his idealism was not discredited or

diminished because he died on German gallows before his
dreams could be realized. For the great fact of the
Christian gospel is that death is not a destructive moment
for us. It is the chance to meet Christ, and if God wills, to
stamp our message even more brilliantly with our blood.
What more can one give? Bonhoeffer, thinking about
these things, wrote:

Daring to do what is right,
Not what fancy may tell you.
Valiantly grasping occasions,
Not cravenly doubting—
Freedom comes only through deed,
Not through thoughts taking wings.

Faint not nor fear,
But go out through the storm and the action,
Trusting in God whose commandment you
*   faithfully follow;*
Freedom exultant will welcome your spirit
*   with joy.*

Frankly I shudder a bit within myself as I make the
choice to join a Bonhoeffer and part company with Mr.
Common-man. I expect to stumble my way through my
daily performance as I attempt to emulate my friends,
Joseph and Isaiah. But do it I will, as a man, as a Christian,
as a pastor, as a husband, as a father, as a friend. And
perhaps even in the attempt I can bring some sort of
honor to the God who has made me. And if you will join
Joseph, Isaiah, myself, and a host of other struggling
witnesses, perhaps we can help each other along the way.

It is not in re-raising the level of the water that we can
bring beauty back to our world. But rather in cleaning up
that which we found to be underneath that makes for
enduring change. This certainly makes a lot of sense to me,
but it can only be accomplished through authentic
charisma, disciplined contemplation, and resolute action.
These are the attributes and actions of persons for
turbulent times.